Anonymous

Anderida

Or, the Briton and the Saxon, A.D. CCCCXLI - Vol. III

Anonymous

Anderida
Or, the Briton and the Saxon, A.D. CCCCXLI - Vol. III

ISBN/EAN: 9783337082727

Printed in Europe, USA, Canada, Australia, Japan

Cover: Foto ©ninatisch / pixelio.de

More available books at **www.hansebooks.com**

ANDERIDA;

OR,

THE BRITON AND THE SAXON

A.D. CCCCXLI.

IN THREE VOLUMES.
VOL. III.

LONDON:
BICKERS AND SON,
1, LEICESTER SQUARE.
1875.

ANDERIDA.

CHAPTER I.

Eomaer's wound, thanks to the efficacy of Tota's charms and a combination of favourable circumstances, was healing so rapidly, that he could get about on crutches. The hay was saved, and stood in noble ricks. The hours had glided pleasantly along, bringing the day which ended Eormenred's leave. To-morrow's dawn must see him in the camp, it being the seventh of his absence. There was no hurry in starting, as nothing would be gained by reaching the river mouth till an hour after noon, when the flood-tide would help them on their way. Setting out five hours after sunrise would give them time enough to reach the river, and go down with the ebb.

All who were to accompany Eormenred were gathered at the Old House, as his farm was named, to share in a farewell meal. The word had been passed, that the king was collecting his strength for a final blow, that Anderida would be taken, and then for a year or two, rest and peace. Consequently, more men were going to the *fyrd* (the national army) than the lands were liable to send. Some came because they wished for peace; some because they wanted plunder; some for the love of fighting, which could not so well be indulged when the war was over. The outlaw, whom no one dare touch while he was in the king's peace in the host, or going to or returning therefrom, hoped by some madly daring act to be inlawed by acclaim of his fellows. Gurhan, who beat his wife, came, as he said, to escape from her tongue. The three sons of Beorlaf came with five friends from the unsettled forest—

silent, solid fellows like themselves, and heavy-handed. Eostrewine had been marching about since daybreak in his brother's harness, which was rather too large to be comfortable, and teazing Leofgifu, who had come with her father, thinking she might be helpful to Geatflæd at such a busy time. Geatflæd showed that she appreciated the attention, and set her future daughter-in-law to scald milk for making clotted cream in a corner of the dairy to which Eomaer could not come with his crutches. The child was so good and biddable, that Geatflæd's heart melted, and allowed her to help in the hall when the guests were seated.

Eomaer watched his sweetheart flitting gracefully here and there; or rather there but not here, for she never came near him, nor looked that way, except when his eyes were in his plate. Vexed at such unexpected fickleness, he took longer pulls at the leathern jack, till Eostrewine, with a tone of superiority, most offensive in a younger brother, said—

"If you go drowning your grief in drink that way, you will anger your wound just for foolishness. I see it all—she keeps looking at you when your head is down among your victuals. You mind what I say, she will be quite different when we men are gone. I know their ways."

Eomaer gazed at his brother with anger and amazement. An impudent, precocious young villain he had always been; but this was a newly assumed form of offence put on with the armour. Since he obtained his father's permission to go to the war he had grown older than his elder brother—that brother one of the king's Gesithas.

"You may stare," Eostrewine continued. "I tell you I know their ways. Didn't they talk before me when I was a youngster; they thought that I was not heeding. Remember the wise saying, 'Fret not thy midriff for a woman, or she will fret it to rags.' They think nothing of a fellow who does not think something of himself. Hold up your head, and she will be more coming on by-and-by, kissing and coaxing and pouting, and all the rest of it."

"You confounded young ass, where did you pick up all that stuff? How dare you speak in that way of a——"

"Ha, ha!" laughed Eostrewine, "that is right, get in a rage. She is looking at you now. Won't we laugh round the camp fire."

"Well," said Eomaer, "in return for all your wise advice take this warning, when you sit by the camp fire with your elders and betters, put a bar on your tongue, or some judicious neighbour may chance to break your head with a marrow-bone."

"Elders and betters! They broke your head, I dare say, but they will not break mine, brother buttermilk. She is looking at——"

The speech was never finished. Backing out of reach of his brother's crutch, Eostrewine bumped up against one of the forest friends of the Beorlafingas, and recoiling as from an oak, with his helmet knocked over his eyes, he ran against a girl carrying scalding pottage, the greater part of which was spilt into his shoes. As he hopped, first on one foot then on the other, he saw that his brother and Leofgifu were laughing at him. That was harder to bear than the scalds, and he was vexed to the soul to find that it was out of his power to retreat with dignity.

The hour of departure was at hand. The leave-takings were brief—shortest perhaps where the pain of parting was deepest.

Geatflæd floured Eostrewine's ankles and bound soft stuff round them. The poor boy was foolish enough to be ashamed of the choking in his throat as he kissed his mother, and could with difficulty make suitable reply to the farewells of Eomaer and Leofgifu, as he limped away to the war.

Eormenred, who brought up the rear of the march, was confronted as he left his own bounds by a wild, ragged figure who dropped from a tree, sprang down the steep bank, and said—

"Let me go with you, Eormenred. You shall not rue it if you do."

"You, Esné," answered the respectable

man, scanning the fierce, vigilant eyes, the tanned, freckled skin, and the tawny, sun-bleached mane of the man before him, "you—flyma and tyhtbysig—a fugitive from justice, a runaway bondman! Have you forgotten that I may kill you where I meet you? Have you no fear of justice?"

"Have you forgotten," Esné answered, "that he who rouses the boar may feel his tusk? I fear! I was never fearful, and now I hold life more cheaply than do the wild swine I harbour with in the forest. I could strangle you, armed as you are, before your friends could help you. But I am not come for any ill end. Let me go with you. I will do you service, make up for the past."

There was a change in the man since Eormenred had last seen him. The eye then dull was bright and clear now; the skin was fine, and had a velvety appearance; the muscles were firmly marked, and the whole frame had the light strength of a wild animal; movements quick without haste or suddenness.

"I see a difference in you," Eormenred said. "What does it mean?"

"It means," answered Esné, showing his strong white teeth, "that there is no ale in the forest, only water, and now I can drink nothing else. I live like a beast, am strong and healthy as a beast. Had I a beast's nature I should be content; but I am a man. I weary of the woods. I yearn for kindly fellowship. I said, Eormenred was good to me long ago; if he will help me once more, I will requite him all in one."

He was the picture of a vagabond, but good fighting stuff if he could be trusted. Eormenred looked at the solid jaw and the firm lips, which the man's young beard could not hide.

"You know the law. If the king will not admit you to his peace, if you be not inlawed, you will be slain there and then."

"I know. Take me with you, and you shall never rue it."

"So be it then. Have you weapons?"

"I have. I will join you on ship-board

ere you leave the river. Esné caught a bough a yard over his head, swung himself into the tree, and vanished. Eormenred shook his head.

"I must keep an eye on him. At all events he is less dangerous with me than prowling about the Mark while we are away."

Eomaer had gone to a hillock not far from the Old House, whence he could have a last view of the departing troop as it wound over a distant slope. He recognised his father, last of them all, by a peculiarity in his walk, the consequence of an old wound. He gave a great sigh, and said aloud—

"Ah, father! I wish I were with you, instead of idling here."

"Oh, Eomaer, you cannot wish that!" exclaimed a voice behind him.

"I can and do wish it," he answered, without looking round.

"But why?" returned the soft, melancholy little voice.

"Because I like being with men, they

know their minds for love or for hate; what they were yesterday they are to-day. Women and girls are otherwise, and I don't like their fickle ways."

"One may feel the same, but not be able to show it."

"When one has any strong feeling the difficulty is to hide it, not to show it. That's how it is with me."

Leofgifu boldly came round in front and took the offensive—

"You only say so to tease; boys love nothing so well as teasing. You are not a bit the same as you were yesterday, not a bit."

"Of course," retorted Eomaer, "if you change, I can't be the same."

"That's how it is with me; if you change, how can I be the same. The question is, who changed first. Is that it?"

"Yes; when I expected you would come and greet me kindly this morning, you kept out of the way—did not speak to me. Then of course I changed, grew dismal. It's the nature of women."

"Ah, to be dismal! No wonder, when we are so badly treated."

"No; to be uncertain—to be glad when they should be sorry, and sorry when they ought to be glad; always unreasonable."

"I'm sorry now," said Leofgifu, pumping up a sigh, "if it is all to end in this way; therefore, of course, I ought to be glad. It was pleasant while it lasted. How long is it since you first loved me?"

"Oh, two or three years," Eomaer answered sulkily.

"Two or three, false boy! If you had loved me at all, you would remember the day, the hour, when so sweet a change came over you."

"Pray how long is it since you first loved me," Eomaer inquired.

"Just one heart-beat after you began to love me. So you see you were the first to change, and all the changes since are entirely your fault. You were wrong in the beginning, you are wrong in the end, and you will never be anything but wrong until you grow wronger. Any message to your mother?"

And Leofgifu performed a little extempore dance round him, singing the while, "Shall I tell his mother, and what shall I tell her?"

"Tell her that I will forgive you, if you give me a kiss."

"Forgive me! When it is all your fault. Kiss you, in such a place as this, where we can be seen for miles. There, as I live, there is somebody over yonder; see how he runs, he goes up the hill like a hare."

"That is Esné," Eomaer told her. "No man can run like him in these parts. He can climb any cliff or tree, and he throws the javelin to hand-breadth at fifty yards, giving it a particular twist."

"I know Esné. He is not so bad as men say. He was hungry once, and I gave him a loaf, afterwards he brought me a nest of young hawks. Father said he risked his life to get the nest, and risked it again in bringing it to me. The hawks died, but that was not his fault. He told me once that I was a pretty little pig, and that he had a mind to carry me off to his cave in the woods, and feed me on acorns and beech-mast till I was fit to eat."

And Leofgifu laughed merrily at the idea of being eaten.

"I would advise him not to talk of eating you, for I mean to eat you myself. I will take a bite out of your nice cheek now."

"That will do. We must go back or your mother will be anxious. Put this arm round me. There—is that as comfortable as the crutch?"

Eormenred, with his fellowship, dropped down the river with the last of the tide, and reached the Mark of the Tortingas about noon. Those left in charge of the ships had got them afloat at high water, and the returning party started immediately. A fair wind and a flowing tide carried them up as far as the old camp (which Ælle had forsaken a few hours previously) a short time before sunset. A boat came off to them with a message from Cymen, and the ships were taken to the point where the fleet lay. Here, in addition to their own galleys, they found Osmund the Jute, brother of Osburh, Ostrythe's mother, with five vessels and over five hundred fighting men. Ælle had promised him a Saxon shilling a day, or a sheep for himself, and the same for every ten men he brought, besides bread, ale, and royal gifts, and they were engaged for forty days at the least.

The arrival of Eormenred, and one or two other ships which had been absent, brought up the whole force, including the Jutes, to more than five thousand men, of whom half were away with the king, seeki g a new camping place, and those who remained with the vessels were employed in building flat-bottomed boats, thirty-six feet long, twelve feet wide, and drawing only a foot and a half of water. These were to be fitted with ladders arranged like those used by Cymen on his first attack, except that each ship was to carry a single ladder, instead of coupled ships carrying two. Many hands make light work; some cut timber to the required shape, some were sawing planks, some placed the floors on the keel, and fixed the kelson in its place with tree-nails, for they had not time to make iron bolts. Others fitted the stem and stern pieces with their knees and aprons, while others plied their adzes on beams, and shelves, and benches. New rope was being stretched, or cut into suitable lengths, and clumsy blocks and dead-eyes were being strapped. Quantities of long, soft moss, suitable for caulking, were spread out to dry, and barrels of pitch and tar from the stores at Wlencing stood in piles here and there. The oars required for the new vessels were being fashioned at the spot where the rafts were made. The banks of this river abounded in ash trees, whence the Saxons named it Ashbourn.

Ælle had formed the design of establishing himself on the northern side of the city and of making himself master of all the water ways which surrounded it, then by completing the destruction of the bridge, he would have the place in his power, and could either starve it or take it by assault as seemed more convenient. The chief difficulty was in finding a dry place. For thousands of years the dirty little river had been bringing soil, and dead leaves, and broken boughs from the forest—filling up one channel, and overflowing into another, while bushes and trees grew everywhere, and helped the land to rise above the water.

Ælle settled on a corner north-east of the city, and just beyond the range of the engines on the walls. He dug trenches twelve feet apart, ordered like the branches of a tree, and threw what was dug out on to the space between, to raise the level. The branches led into a main trunk with a floating door which closed as the tide rose, and opened when it fell.

The men worked so long as daylight lasted, then making fires of the brushwood they had cleared away, they cooked their supper on the embers. The smaller twigs were spread on the ground, and all but the sentries slept serenely.

CHAPTER II.

AFTER the scene in the basilica the bishop returned with Vortipore to the palace, where, over some old Gallic wine, they took serious counsel concerning the Count's interests. The bishop was too patriotic, too straightforward to be told his friend's inmost thought —the feeling that Anderida might as well perish (so far as the Count's affairs were concerned) as be saved by Julius. Such a notion would have been scouted as unworthy, but there were not many things the prelate would refuse to do in order to save his accustomed friend, and his friend's position. His best advice was assuredly not to be denied to Vortipore, and the counsel was not likely to be slighted.

In consequence of their deliberations Vortipore, on the following morning, went from one old confederate to another, suiting his discourse to the temper of each. Beginning with indifferent topics, he worked round to his object, found no difficulty in demonstrating that if such or such a course had been adopted, results differing from actual events would have ensued, and as actual events were about as unpleasant as could be, it was easy to suppose that the different results might have been more agreeable. Then something would remind the Count of a past adventure in which himself and his interlocutor had been engaged. The exploit was not necessarily a very creditable one, but it was invariably lively, and lost nothing in the reminiscence, while even the little fictions which embellished it somehow drew the two men more closely together. Such recollections often tell more weightily than real service and sacrifice.

It was with Madoc that Vortipore was most anxious to renew the old feeling of comradeship. An exile from Calleva, he had been received by the Count of the Saxon Shore, in the first instance out of dislike to the ruler of Calleva, but Madoc proved so useful and ready, that a friendship sprang up between the two men which nothing could destroy, so long as mutual advantages might be expected. But though Madoc had acquired wealth through his favour with the Count, so that he was able to maintain a force of from four to five hundred men in his service, he wished for a fair opportunity of deserting the falling cause, and of making his peace with the Count of Calleva.

Vortipore deemed it an evil omen when he saw Madoc wavering in his friendship, and his earliest visit was to his old ally.

They spoke of the burning of the bridge, and Vortipore remarked—

"It is a grave disaster, and one which might have been averted by the most ordinary knowledge of the rules of war. I do not blame the Praefect for his want of experience in military affairs, but I do condemn the rash conceit which leads him to rely on his inexperience. A venial error becomes criminal when its consequence, instead of merely injuring the individual, ruins the state."

"It is a question whether any skill and practice in warfare could have warded off those fire-rafts. We had certain knowledge that the design to attack from below was serious, though it was afterwards made as a feint only."

"My good friend," said Vortipore, laying his hand gently on the other's arm, "I know your generous temper of old. You would palliate a blunder you yourself are incapable of committing. If the chief direction had been in your hands, the bridge would have been protected above as well as below. Any part left defenceless invites the enemy's blow. But granting that the danger could not be foreseen in time to guard the bridge effectually, what was to prevent a detachment of boats destroying the rafts, or towing them to the bank, as was done on the western shore. Twelve or fourteen of the small craft would have sufficed for the purpose, and enough would have remained to encounter the Saxons with a force superior to their own. I saw the mistake, but could not get it rectified."

As this error was Madoc's own, he, in his eagerness to engage the Saxons, having forgotten part of the duties assigned to him, there was some difficulty in explaining it in a graceful manner.

"It was an oversight, doubtless," he said, "but I am far from taking such an unfavourable view of our condition as some do. With a little dash, a little good management, and a little good luck, the Saxons might be made very uncomfortable in their muddy labyrinth. I do not quite see how to do it, but——"

"It is to be done," cried Vortipore, "and I can tell you how to do it; but first of all, there are certain discontents to be appeased. There is Farinmail, he has been neglected through my fault, or rather it would be more proper to call it my ill luck."

"Better call it a fault," Madoc answered coldly; "a fault may be amended, but it is useless trying to help an unlucky man."

"Fault it shall be then, and amended it shall be. Bronwen and he shall be brought together. We will bury the Saxons in the swamp, and finish the war with a wedding. By this time next year I may be a grandfather. How the years slip away. It was but yesterday that you and I watched for the child in the opening of the forest, as the pilgrims went toward London to Archbishop Guitolinus. How amazed they were to be set upon in such a place!—What a spot it was!"

"Yes, truly. Well may men call the forest 'an tred.'* Not a house nor a human being did we see for thirty miles, except ourselves and our two servants, till the pilgrims came up."

"We did not see much then. How dark it was! It was your device of filling the guide's flask with strong wine that delayed

* Andred, from "an tred," without habitation.—*Guest.*

them. I never think without sorrow of the death of the nurse. What a faithful old creature she was! How she held the child!"

"An old fool!" said Madoc harshly. "No one wanted to hurt her, or the child either. If we had not been so pressed for time——"

"We were pressed for time," said Vortipore with a laugh, "but not so pressed as we were the next morning, when the archbishop's men so nearly caught us snoring. It would have proved an awkward business if you had not so adroitly led them into the bog. How we laughed at them!"

"Ha, ha, ha!" laughed Madoc. "What a pickle they were in! But it was your fancy to drag them out one by one, bind their arms behind their backs, and bid them walk home to their master as their horses were mired. What a procession it was. Shall I ever laugh so again?"

"That you shall. Do you remember the pleasant penance our good bishop enjoined— The venison in its season, and the grape that is ripe?"

"The grapes were ripe assuredly, and so were some others—eh, Madoc?"

"They were. And the answer he sent to Guitolinus," replied Madoc. "Ha, ha, ha!—the two reverend fathers and his four penitent children. Snow has fallen on our heads since then, and ice creeps about our hearts."

"No, no!" Vortipore exclaimed, "it is not winter yet—a summer storm, a frost in June. The storm will pass, the hailstones that hang in our beards will melt, and we will laugh as blithely as ever. Come to me to-night, and we will discuss my plan. Now—farewell."

The Count then went in quest of Farinmail, whom he hoped to mollify without much trouble. He took his way through the Forum, one corner of which he found to be obstructed by a crowd gathered round Renatus, who was speaking in a rapid, somewhat incoherent manner. His hearers had a perplexed look, as if the thread of the discourse were slipping from their hands.

He had been blaming those who doubted and denied the visions and prophecies of the seer.

"You see not," he cried; "you hear not! Satan and the Saxon are at your throats, but you heed not. You hold up your little lamps, and swear with a slumberous yawn that all is dumbness and endless night. How should blind moles, toiling in the pit, know of flowers, and bright skies, and carolling birds? Ah, there are sounds which make no music in your ears, there are rays to which your eyes are dull; but the infinite, void darkness is populous day to senses keener and of wider range. Were a little of your earthiness withdrawn you also would see visions, hear the ineffable; would behold the multitude of the heavenly host; would listen to the song of flaming-hearted seraphim—choral voices of the morning stars hymning, 'Glory to God in the highest.' Earth, earth, drags us down. For me—fierce beasts howl in the dens below, serpents writhe in the outer gloom; the light is the glow of the burning lake, where every moment millions and millions of sparks fly aloft, each spark a human soul; they turn and fall again into the seething lava—memories of folly, vanity, sin—while the boundless anguish goes up as a roaring flame to heaven for ever and ever. Chasten your bodies with vigil and fast, strengthen your souls by meditation and prayer, then may you hope to discern holy things"—(at this point, the speaker's eye fell on the Count, with his attendants pushing through the crowd, and he added, with sudden fierceness)—" and persons; discern—I say, holy things and persons from such as are impure and vile. When you see a great one of the earth pass by with symbols of rank and power on his head and in his hand, the ministers of his pride and lust at his heels, you will at the same time behold in his heart the image of the fiend on whose altar he sacrifices the honour of women, the innocence of children, the faith and valour of men. There is an altar in your heart, Vortipore, an altar with hot coals, and blood and bones of victims; but the image of the fiend to whom they are offered, the hideous, ruthless Moloch-idol, is none other than yourself."

Vortipore looked on the man he had wronged, and cursed the feeling which made him shrink from the challenge. With an effort he replied—

"Look in your own breast, mad monk. Is the image you see there a pleasant one to contemplate? The heart of another man is a sealed book, it is your own shadow you look upon."

Then, with a smile to the citizens around, the Count went on—

"None but a fool resents the words of a madman, but I think it would be better for himself if this fellow were in confinement. His railing tongue will get him into mischief. Does any one know where he comes from? His speech shows he is not a Briton."

Renatus disappeared, but the crowd stood discussing his merits.

"He may be mad, or a foreigner, or what

you will," said a critic, "but how finely he speaks. That 'burning lake' now!"

The bishop, on his way to the Basilica, was hindered by the crowd, and heard several praising the eloquence of Renatus—

"Look down that street," he cried; "do you see the pig which has escaped from the butcher and his lad? Now the lad gets hold of an ear, the butcher seizes the other, and the pig is fast. Wise men judge by deeds. You are caught by the ears like the fugitive pig."

The men laughed, and looked after their pastor with mingled feelings.

"He is no foreigner," one said, "nor mad; but what then, more is wanted than that surely. He cannot preach movingly to my mind."

"He can tell you you are a fool," another cried. "Wise men do this, you do the absolute contrary, and you may draw the conclusion for yourselves."

"He never catches men's ears by fine phrases," a third remarked; "but I do not remember any fine deeds to judge him by. He can hunt, and he can drink, and they say he can do other things unbefitting a bishop."

"He can strike hard when he sees occasion," was the observation of a fourth, "and so can his sub-deacons. I was glad to get out of the Basilica last night with whole bones. It was more than some did."

But on the whole, the bishop was liked by most of the citizens.

Renatus, meantime, was falling into that state of mind which allows evil to be thought of, though not with approval. Excuses might be made for one who did such a thing, he considered, though he would not be guilty of it himself, even under the greatest provocation. The temptation to help on the fulfilment of his own prediction concerning the destruction of the city, was growing strong. The allotted time was speeding away, twenty days had elapsed, and much remained to be done. The Saxons, destitute of engines for siege-work, would be detained long before these strong walls; the city was well provisioned, nothing but treachery could give them entrance.

He sat lonely in his bare cell, and Vortipore's words recurred to his memory with envenomed sting. His mind was losing its lucidity—its concentration on the matter in hand. He sometimes woke up in the midst of his discourse, as a charioteer might who had nodded over his reins when the road was smooth, and found his speech had turned into a by-way. In spite of watching and fast, the naked, wild-eyed human beast in the secret chamber of his heart became more evident, indeed it was most rampant after the most rigorous self-discipline. What if he should lose the faculty of discriminating between right and wrong; fall into sin, imperil his soul, discredit his cause—the cause of truth and righteousness. Would it not be better to fly to the desert, and end his days in solitude? Solitude!—the man-beast would be with him in the desert. Better far to put off this earth-soiled garment once for all. A crucifix hung against the blank, stained wall—a gaunt, agonized, white figure on a dark cross. He too had worn the earthly garment, had assumed it of his free will, had undergone all that can be suffered—anguish of mind, torture of body, suggestions of the fiend—and was now at God's right hand watching with eyes of tender sympathy His struggling followers. Renatus clutched the image and bound it on his breast, so that, howsoever his thoughts might stray, each movement of his body should remind him of the mighty Deliverer. He prostrated himself on the ground, and cried long and earnestly for deliverance in temptation. By-and-by he rose, took bread, filled his gourd with water, and set out for Pen y Coit.

Vortipore, chewing the cud of Renatus' remark and of his own answer, vowed that he would put an end to such insolent attacks. Passing through the great gate, he met Julius, and stopped to speak to him.

"I wish, Lord Praefect, you had heard the mad monk, just now."

"Just now, Lord Count, I have matters in hand more pressing than the utterances of mad monks, or even of sane ones."

"Doubtless you think them so, but you sometimes form erroneous judgments as to the relative importance of circumstances, as also of persons. I warn you, officially, that this fellow is stirring up the multitude against the civil authority, using language calculated to excite insurrection; and I require you, in the interest of order and good government, to take measures which shall prevent his doing mischief."

"Lord Count, the seclusion of your life has perhaps caused you to be imperfectly informed concerning the events of the last few days. The man to whom I suppose you refer, is by no means disaffected, on the contrary, he has recently given evidence of wise zeal for the public good. As to the private griefs of which you have heretofore spoken, your devotion to the cause of Britain will, I am sure, tell you that this is no time to search into them, but that every man and every energy should be dedicated to the common weal."

Something in this speech moved the Count to greater fury than the attack made upon him in public, by Renatus, had evoked. His face flushed, his hands clenched themselves as he spoke—

"Well, Lord Praefect, we shall see—we shall see whether my authority is to be disputed, my person insulted with impunity. The defiance you offer is accepted, and the quarrel shall be settled in another arena."

"I offer neither insult nor defiance," Julius answered calmly; "and as to your quarrel with the monk, if you require me to investigate it in my official capacity, of course it is my duty to do so."

But the Count was out of hearing. He had turned back to the gate, feeling too nettled for an interview with Farinmail. Instead of a personal invitation to each, he sent missives, calling the chiefs who were likely to favour his project to the council-table that evening.

At the entrance of the palace, he was met by the ugliest youth that ever existed, Morvran, the son of Tegid.

"What do you want?" Vortipore asked, with unrestrained pettishness.

"Tegid, your servant and kinsman greets you. He has gathered more than forty of your old tenants, now slaves in the hands of the Saxons. They will gladly serve their old master again, and will bring not less than a score more, but they require arms—swords and bucklers at the least—for the Saxons who hold your lands are suspicious, and would cut them to pieces at the first movement if they have no means of defence. One cart-load of weapons will be enough."

"Will it?" said Vortipore; "then I shall not send it. Do you go, and if the heathen oppose the retreat of my men, do you display the terrors of your countenance, and they will fly like birds."

"Is that the answer I am to take to my father, Lord Count?"

"Yes. The Saxons will take you for the devil, and avoid you as such."

So Morvran went back to his father, and the Count lost the services of both; but men still say, even to this day, 'as ugly as Morvran-ap-Tegid, whom no one struck in battle because they thought he was the devil.' Tegid, and the men he had recruited, joined the Count of Calleva, who loved them for the good service they did.

About sunset the invited chiefs met in the main court of the palace, each of them bringing with him ten or a dozen followers, picked men and well armed. After slight consultation they all entered the council-room, and their attendants gathered around the door, about fourscore men in all.

Vortipore, who was writing at a table, rose as they entered, and after a few courteous words to each, addressed them—

"Lords, friends, and fellow-warriors, our state is such at this moment that no apology is needed for troubling you with frequent meetings. It were an insult, after all you have done, to suppose that you grudge your time, your blood, or your lives in the cause of our country. The matters I would now submit to your consideration are three: one concerning myself; one having reference to our noble ally, Lord Farinmail, whom I hope soon to greet by a dearer title."

Farinmail stirred uneasily on his seat, like a man who knows that the time for something unpleasant is near.

"The third is a proposal for the relief of the city. I shall invert the order in which they were mentioned, as public interests take precedence of private ones, however urgent.

"You know, lords, how the enemy, after many shiftings, has betaken himself to the marshy lands eastward of the city. My plan is to take advantage of the night tide, and throwing five thousand men across the water, to catch them unprepared, perhaps divided, and extirpate them; deal a heavy blow at least."

"Where do you think of landing?" asked Etlym Red-sword.

"That is a matter of detail, there are many places."

"But not many landing places," said Etlym. "With the boats we have it will be two hours' work, and more, to get five thousand men across; meantime the fall of the tide will make it impossible to land at any place I am acquainted with."

"How many men has Ælle, and how distributed?" Cadogan inquired.

"That," replied Vortipore, "is a mystery which we can solve to-morrow."

"Why not send for the Praefect and solve it to-night?" asked Elphin. "How is it that he is not here? His presence is necessary."

"Not necessary by any means," said the Count, losing his patience rapidly; "not even desirable, until the second branch of my address has been considered, as that refers to a personal matter between myself and him. It is in fact an accusation of no light kind which duty compels me to bring against him."

"In his absence!" Gower exclaimed— "absurd. We shall entertain no secret charge against Julius Romanus. We shall not quarrel with our shield in the heat of the battle. We should be fools, or traitors."

"Our shield!" cried Cadogan, "say, rather, our right hand, for he alone grasps all the threads of our operations for offence or defence."

"And how came you," the Count burst in angrily, "how dare you allow this man to usurp such powers, powers which are mine? How could you suffer my rights to be invaded, my authority to be superseded?"

"Ay!" said old Gower coolly. "Now you ask a sensible question; one that goes to the root of the matter. You left us to shift for ourselves, and we had to do as well as we could without you."

"That is so," said Elphin. "This is no war for glory or territory. The fate of Regnum is impending over our heads. We shall be utterly effaced, as when one smooths from a tablet a name of no further import to make room for another. You are Count of the Saxon Shore—now reduced to the space under the city wall—and in the extremity of the danger you shut yourself up in your palace, refusing to see any of us. We choose the most capable man in this extremity, and invest him with the function yon have abdicated."

"Which I have not abdicated," thundered the Count, "as you shall learn to your cost. Guards, arrest these men as traitors!"

But as his guards came in by one door, the followers of the recusant chiefs entered by another; either side shrank from the responsibility of bloodshed, and no sword was drawn as yet.

"Farinmail my son, Madoc old friend, you will stand by me. Etlym Red-sword, it is not your wont to forsake the weaker party."

"You have slept too long," was all the reply that Etlym made.

"You are unlucky, it is useless to help you," Madoc answered.

"Lord Count," Farinmail said, "I decline the honour you proposed to confer on me for reasons which I will explain to you in private, if you require them, but I hope sincerely that you will not."

"See that your reasons are good and sufficient. Require them! That will I, and pluck them out of your false, cowardly throat. Require them! Yes, if you hide yourself under your father's chair."

Farinmail's brown cheek burned, but he only said, "I shall not hide."

There was a bustle behind the chiefs, men stood aside, and Julius came forward with several scrolls in his hand, together with a parchment, from which hung a broad, massive seal.

"Lords," the Praefect began, "a runner has arrived from Caer Emrys with despatches, one of which is so important that, although it is addressed to myself, I think it due to you that it should be opened in your presence. Observe, I pray, that seal and cord are untouched."

The seal was recognised as that of the Pendragon, who lay wounded at Caer-lion upon Usk, near which river the hostile forces were face to face, but in a condition too exhausted to fight.

The Pendragon wrote bitterly. The efforts of brave and able men were frustrated by childish folly and selfishness. Vortipore should no more exercise powers which he had abused. He was to be deprived of his dignity and cast into prison, while a council, presided over by Julius, should administer the affairs of the district for the present. Let them do their best, for in thirty days the Pendragon would relieve them.

Vortipore looked round to his guards, one or two closed up to him, but most hung their heads. He looked at his friends, who avoided his gaze. He unbuckled his belt, and said to Julius—

"Lord Praefect, *you* are an open foe. You need not blush to take my sword."

CHAPTER III.

Ælle stood on the bank looking toward Anderida, studying the defences, pondering whether it was worth while to destroy the stakes on that side and so to open the channel to his ships. It would not cost much to do it, and he could afford to sacrifice a few men, since Osmund the Jute came and announced that other reinforcements were on their way. He would soon be able to count man for man with the enemy, and that was long odds in favour of the Saxons; but he was not disposed to waste such good material as his army contained; the greater his strength the more he could accomplish. The engines on the walls disturbed his calculations. They were more formidable than he had believed; but so much of their efficacy depended on the skill with which they were handled, that he could arrive at no certain conclusion.

The tide rose, covering the muddy shore; the men were preparing to launch the boats which had been hauled up for security the night before; the various noises of the camp mingled with sound of axes echoing in the wood; various officers stood awaiting his commands, but still the king stood stiff and immovable as a pollard oak, unable to answer the question, "Is it worth while to open the passage?"

A boat came pulling across the shining water to a rough jetty which projected, in a half-finished state, over the mud to a floating stage. The boat was made fast to this stage and two men landed, bringing with them a prisoner whose arms were fastened behind him by leathern thongs at the elbows. Ælle turned his head as the men drew near.

"Who is this?" he asked. "Why is he brought to me?"

"He came to the other bank of the Ashbourn this morning, and cried to us that he had tidings for you. He would not tell us what they are, though we threatened him with torture—and indeed gave him a little taste of it—so we bring him to you."

"That you should have done at first," Ælle said angrily. "It is not for you to maltreat those who come of their free will to serve us. Cut his bonds and withdraw out of hearing that we may speak without restraint. Now, Welshman, what is it?"

"I am no Briton, but a borderer. Corr is my name. I have done the king some slight service heretofore, and have tasted of his bounty. Moreover, I have been cruelly wronged by my—by the Count of the Saxon Shore—and his people. See, Lord King, the scars are even now scarcely healed on my back and wrists."

"I see you have been scourged sufficiently," Ælle said, as Gorr pulled the greasy doublet from his back and showed the marks.

"As if that was not enough, they left me tied up to a tree and went away after the white hart, for not finding which——"

"Send for Ent!" the king shouted to an officer. "I know who you are now and will avenge your wrongs, though it seems that you require my assistance rather than bring me information." As Ælle spoke he drew down his shaggy brows till the eyes were almost concealed, but Gorr saw they watched him keenly.

"If the news I bring enables you to crush your enemies I am revenged. Judge you of its worth. The holy man who found me and healed my hurts, had intelligence brought him by a rascally charcoal-burner early this morning, and desired me to carry it to Anderida, as it is of the highest importance. I obeyed from motives of gratitude; but the memory is more tenacious of wrongs than of kindness, and I bring this message to you. For my reward I only ask this—that you will patiently hear and weigh a plan I shall propose for your advantage."

"I will hear patiently, but do not be too long-winded in the telling."

"Briefly then: a fresh army of Britons is advancing against you from the north-west, and encamped last night some thirty miles from this place. The forest men are thronging to join it."

"That is news indeed," said Ælle. Then, after a pause, "It is not the custom among the Britons to trust matters of consequence to word of mouth. You have runes, do not compel me to find them."

Gorr knew that not only his clothes would be examined, but his body cut in pieces in the search for the letter, which his quailing eye had told the king was about his person.

"It was not in my mind to conceal anything from the eagle eyes of my Lord the King, I am not so foolish. It is that this scroll is written in magic characters, which have no meaning to me, nor to any as I suppose, but the man to whom they are sent."

Protesting his honesty with many oaths, Gorr ripped open a seam of his doublet, and produced a strip of vellum, on which was inscribed a sentence whose language was Latin, but the character Greek.

Ælle turned the document this way and that, and sent for Cnebba.

Meantime Ent arrived, and casting his eyes on Gorr, exclaimed—

"A word in your ear, Lord King. Do not trust that man; he would cheat me, if he could. False to both sides he is."

"See what you can get out of him," said the king. "Can you tell me what this means? Is it dangerous to keep?"

"Some infernal spell, no doubt; but I had better look after Gorr. I could easily find out the meaning, if I had time."

The king sent for the swiftest runners in his camp, and dispatched them in a north-westerly direction, with warning to be alert.

Cnebba appeared, the magnificent organ to which he owed his name cleaving the air before him. He was a long, lean man, who walked with his body bent stiffly forward. His eyebrows turned up, and his mouth turned down, while an extraordinary squint imparted a sort of uncanny look to his countenance. He had been a captive among the Britons, and had picked up, during a long period of servitude, the rudiments of reading, writing, and demonology. To this latter art he was indebted for his escape from slavery, having set fire to the farm in an unsuccessful attempt to raise the devil, and frightened his master into the well.

He owed his fame as a soothsayer chiefly to his quick hearing and his retentive memory; but he believed that he was aided by the devil, whom he hoped by persevering effort some day to call up in a visible form. In the course of his researches he had learned several useful secrets respecting the properties of various herbs, salts, and animal substances, and had become a tolerable ventriloquist, and a highly accomplished mimic.

Into the hand of this man of science was given the mystic scroll—

KOMITICKΑΛΛΗΒΑΕΚΑCTPΑṮW
NYNTPΠPOΠEΠENYKOITMMMK
OMITANTIBYCBENIT.

Ent had been trying, with no great success, to probe the motive of his companion. Gorr repeated his story with great accuracy, but gave short answers when pressed on other points. He would communicate his plan to none but the king, both because betrayal would endanger his life, and a secret is no secret when told to a third person; and also because he would keep for himself any profit which might accrue from the execution of the scheme. Accordingly, Gorr now reminded the king of his promise, and was forthwith vouchsafed a hearing.

The plan was that the slippery forester was to be kept in confinement, according to all outward appearance, but in fact allowed to escape with the missive of Renatus sewn up in his doublet as before. He was to swim across to the city, and present himself dripping at the gate, deliver the note to Julius, and tell that he had been taken by the Saxons, but had escaped before they could wring his secret from him. Then he would return to the Saxon camp as soon as there was any movement of the Britons which seemed of importance.

A slight modification, however, had to be made in this arrangement. Cnebba had disappeared with the manuscript entrusted to him. He had last been seen in the outskirts of the forest, running like a fowl, with his head far in advance of his legs, and a glow of satisfaction on his saturnine visage. He had once before beheld similar characters in a book belonging to a very learned clerk, and had been told by the slave who showed it to him that by its aid his master controlled fiends, bent the powers of nature to his will, eclipsed both sun and moon, foretold future events, and detected thieves. This fragment most probably possessed like virtues, and in a little hut, devoted to experiments in the

Into the hand of this man of science was given the mystic scroll—

ΚΟΜΙΤΙΟΚΑΛΛΗΒΛΕΚΑΟΤΡΑΤΤΩ
ΝΥΝΤΡΠΡΟΠΕΠΕΝΥΚΟΙΤΜΜΝΚ
ΟΜΙΤΑΝΤΙΒΥΟΒΕΝΙΤ.

Ent had been trying, with no great success, to probe the motive of his companion. Gorr repeated his story with great accuracy, but gave short answers when pressed on other points. He would communicate his plan to none but the king, both because betrayal would endanger his life, and a secret is no secret when told to a third person; and also because he would keep for himself any profit which might accrue from the execution of the scheme. Accordingly, Gorr now reminded the king of his promise, and was forthwith vouchsafed a hearing.

The plan was that the slippery forester was to be kept in confinement, according to all outward appearance, but in fact allowed to escape with the missive of Renatus sewn up in his doublet as before. He was to swim across to the city, and present himself dripping at the gate, deliver the note to Julius, and tell that he had been taken by the Saxons, but had escaped before they could wring his secret from him. Then he would return to the Saxon camp as soon as there was any movement of the Britons which seemed of importance.

A slight modification, however, had to be made in this arrangement. Cnebba had disappeared with the manuscript entrusted to him. He had last been seen in the outskirts of the forest, running like a fowl, with his head far in advance of his legs, and a glow of satisfaction on his saturnine visage. He had once before beheld similar characters in a book belonging to a very learned clerk, and had been told by the slave who showed it to him that by its aid his master controlled fiends, bent the powers of nature to his will, eclipsed both sun and moon, foretold future events, and detected thieves. This fragment most probably possessed like virtues, and in a little hut, devoted to experiments in the wondrous light, and reciting charms to render it propitious. Then he withdrew into the hut, which was formed of poles, with branches tied on them the thin ends downward. There was a hole in the top for the escape of smoke, and immediately under the opening, a rusted brazier stood crankily on its three legs. He lighted a charcoal fire in the tripod, and as it burned up clear, he caused his voice to issue from various points, above and below, summoning the fiends to his presence. Then he threw on the fire the herbs, and other matters he had collected, which produced a most detestable smell. By the light of the burning weeds, he shouted aloud such combinations of letters as he could make out on the parchment, changing their order in hopes of discovering the spell. Nothing came of it, but he refused to be discouraged, growing more excited and clamorous as the time wore away. Voices of beasts and birds, mingled with groans and ejaculations, filled the air as he gashed his cheeks and breast, and cast the blood on the earth and in the fire. At last, as he was rehearsing an incantation, derived by many descents from a noted sorcerer of old, he heard a voice, not his own, growling deeply from the other side of the hut. Continuing his efforts without any relaxation, he bent his long body on one side, and distinctly saw the light of the brazier reflected from the eyes of some creature, whose head was buried among the leafy walls. It was a critical moment. " Erochnal faminabosti," cried Cnebba, and with increased growling, a terrible head and a huge, hairy arm were thrust from under the boughs. " Nehushti marfas," shrieked the wizard, and before the words had left his lips the hut shook, sparks flew in the air, and a grim, weird being, unlike the sons of men, lay on the floor of the tabernacle. Cnebba thrilled with rapturous horror as he recognised its resemblance to the traditional earth-demon. "Goreen, goreeja, goristan," he yelled, as he scattered fresh blood on the monster, which rose up and uttered unearthly sounds.

So far all had been an unbroken success, every step according with the tradition handed down, but now the artist was moved to try an innovation. Holding the parchment over the brazier, he read—it was all he could read—" Kom, pon, ben." The monster seized him by the throat with strangling clutch, and snatched away the vellum.

"Ah, master," gasped Cnebba, with choked utterance.

"You have broken the charm," the deep voice said, "insulted the powers of the earth, but I will spare your life on one condition."

"Cursed be the day that I got that unlucky, that evil spell."

"The spell is good if rightly used. Tell me how you came by it."

"A forester brought it to the camp; a man with a back scarred as——"

"You speak of this," exclaimed the fiend, holding out the parchment. "Go on, I know all about it, but I would learn if you are fit to be spared."

Cnebba had not much to tell, which

his supernatural antagonist was not slow to ascertain, and having other business on hand, spoke thus—

"For this time I release you, but before you rise, you must repeat ten times these words, 'goriolowak negus Bael,' to appease the other powers."

Cnebba was dashed to the ground, the earth-demon kicked over the brazier, and disappeared with a terrible crash. The prostrate artist endeavoured to repeat the prescribed words, but the brazier was blistering his legs, the hut was catching fire from the scattered coals, and he rushed out of the door. But heart and knees failed him then, for a burst of mocking laughter echoed from the forest. Not till morning sun arose dared he return, limping and crest-fallen, to the Saxon camp, where the tale of horror he related, confirmed as it was by the marks of the demon's hot feet, mightily increased his reputation.

Bael met Julius at the usual point on the bridge, and made a report of all he had observed. In conclusion he gave a strip of vellum, saying, "A man with a scarred back brought this to Ælle sixteen hours ago."

"This to Ælle!" Julius said with astonishment "these are no Saxon runes."

"No one could read them. I found a conjurer in the forest trying to raise a demon to interpret them. I happened to know the spell."

Bael laughed, but Julius was busy trying to read the characters.

"Count of Calleva—camp pitched near Pen y Coit. I wish the moon would give a better light. One, two, three thousand; this must be from Renatus—Pen y coit—I cannot read the last part by this light. Was the man who brought this to Ælle a prisoner?"

"The conjurer thought he was. Here is something more. A man came swimming from the direction of the Saxon camp. He moved his shoulders as if they hurt him, perhaps the salt water made his back smart. About fifty yards from the place where he landed—yonder—he rose up in the water and threw away his cap; he sank after throwing it, and did not see that the cap floated where it fell. It seemed odd to throw away his cap just before he came ashore. I picked it up, ripped open the lining, and found a folded parchment. Here it is."

"Why this," said Julius, "is a copy of the other; at least"—and he examined part of the inscription which had not been damaged by the water—"such an imitation as a person ignorant of the Greek character might be supposed to make. But why should he do it?"

"The other was lost," Bael suggested; "conjurer had it, don't you see?"

"And if this were found, with the writing effaced by the water, it would confirm his story. The man is an ingenious fool. I must see him."

Half an hour afterwards Gorr was telling his story to the Praefect.

"So in swimming across you had the misfortune to lose your cap."

"I was so unfortunate, Lord Praefect, and what was worse, the writing in it; but I beg you to consider my exhausted condition. I had tasted nothing since sunrise, the way was difficult, and in my anxiety to make speed I overdid it, being weak from recent illness."

"What was the nature of your indisposition?" Julius asked.

"I suffered from the effects of exposure and ill treatment. I had been robbed and beaten, left tied to a tree for many hours. The holy man——"

"Ah, I have heard something of that business. Vortipore is your enemy, as he has been mine. It is well that you came to me."

"Yes, Lord Praefect, that is what I said to Renatus. Said I——"

"Yes, yes, you spoke very wisely, but we will pass over that; go on about yourself. You were weak from recent illness."

"I felt as if a cup of wine would do me good, but none was there."

"There is none here," said Julius, "get on, and perhaps you may deserve some."

Gorr thought how good-natured this man

was whom he had heard spoken of as so terrible, and went on with confidence—

"Well, for my ease, I turned on my back, the tide being in my favour, and doing so the cap fell off; that is all about it."

"Not quite all," said the good-natured man, throwing a wet furry thing on the table. "Not quite all. Is that your cap?"

"N—n—no," Gorr stammered, "that is, it is very like it. I can't say——"

"If it is yours the despatch will be inside it, I suppose."

"Ye—yes, I suppose—that is, if no one has taken it out."

"Precisely," the Praefect observed; "you speak like a book. Is it there?"

Gorr began to wish he had not been so ingenious. The cap had floated crown uppermost, and the top was comparatively dry. If only part of the parchment should prove to be uninjured—and he could not think, with those unwinking eyes fixed on him?

"Why do you not ascertain if the despatch is there?"

"Lord Praefect, I am afraid—yes, my knife is lost as well."

An arm reached over his shoulder, a hand placed a knife on the table—his own knife —still wet. Gorr wished himself out of this uncanny room, he opened the knife, cut some stitches, and said—

"There is something inside here, Lord Praefect, and I dare say it is my cap, but I ought to mention that this despatch—I hope it is all right—but I have not seen it; it was inserted by another person."

"You know nothing about it then; it may be nonsense for anything you know. Did Renatus tell you what he had written about?"

"He said he had written in magic characters which no one would understand. He did not tell me anything about the contents."

"Renatus does not seem to trust you so completely as you deserve."

"He is peculiar, Lord Praefect, queer in the head, and has been worse than usual lately. Here is the writing and may all the curses of heaven fall on my head if I know anything—Why—what—what is this? Merciful heaven forgive! Oh, what does it mean?"

The manuscript which unfolded itself in Gorr's shaking hand was not his own clumsy forgery, but the clear black letters of the original document which he knew very well, though he could neither read nor imitate them. Here, in his hand, was the parchment which the sorcerer had carried away into the forest. Had it been replaced by magic, or was he betrayed? He looked across to Julius, who held in his hand a similar piece of vellum.

"Perhaps we had better make an exchange," the Praefect said. "Your parchment seems to trouble you, and mine is incomprehensible."

The two pieces were changed accordingly, and Gorr received his own arrangement of scratches arbitrarily composed.

"This," said Julius, "is perfectly intelligible; but there are one or two other matters which require explanation, and I advise you to furnish a solution of certain mysteries at once. If you have any statement or proposal to make, there is an official who will attend to you; or if you desire to see a priest you can do so."

"What does it mean?" Gorr asked the jailer who led him away.

"Mean! It means you are going to the torture-chamber."

"But the proposal—what can I do? I will consent to anything. What is expected of me? My head is too giddy for me to think."

"I cannot tell," the jailer answered. "But here we are. Will you have a priest?"

Presently the jailer came out to attend to his other business, and the thick doors closed upon Gorr.

CHAPTER IV.

The Saxon runners returned in the evening of the day they were sent, bringing confirmation of the report that a considerable British force was within a few leagues of the camp. The scouts had not been able to approach this force closely, as its front was covered by swarms of forest men—strong, hardy fellows, skilful with bow and javelin, who eat more of the flesh of the deer and wild boar than of the domesticated breeds of animals. Several of Ælle's men fell into the hands of these hunters, and were not heard of again. This was all the intelligence they could gather.

The Saxon king sent Cissa, his son, with five hundred men, to push aside these skirmishers, and ascertain the real force which was coming against him; but the Ætheling was on no account to hazard an engagement, he was to return as soon as possible. Ælle feared that behind these foresters was the Pendragon with all the strength of Lloegyr * at his back. If it were so he must choose his ground for fighting, and do nothing rashly. He was most anxious for the return of Gorr from the city, but Gorr came not. Cissa marched in the morning as soon as it was light enough to see his way; and bridges of boats were constructed to carry him over the two main streams.

The Ætheling divided his force into twenty bodies of twenty-five men each, which were to keep near enough to each other for mutual support, and were to thread their way, as they best could, through the woods and marshes which covered all that region.

Cissa had not long been gone when Smith made his appearance in the camp. Up to

* The great divisions of Britain were Alban, the North; Cymru, the West; and Lloegyr, the South.—*Guest.*

this time he had remained in Anderida, concealed in the house of Rhys; but the dangers and difficulties both for himself and his friend had increased so much since the stricter Julius had replaced Vortipore, that it was considered better that Smith should withdraw. He had left copies of the keys of the postern with Rhys, and had arranged a method of communicating with him at stated times.

Smith said that the report ran in Anderida that the Pendragon was badly wounded, but that succours were hoped for from Emyr, Count of Calleva. Being asked if he had heard anything of Gorr, who had been told to communicate with him, Smith said at first that he had not; but afterwards it struck him that he had overheard some talk of a spy being caught and tortured. Smith thought the spy must have been Gorr who confessed.

"As of course he would to save his own dirty carcase; and so when I came near the house, it was lucky that I stopped to see that all was clear. There were men lurking here and there, sent, no doubt, to look out for me in consequence of Gorr's confession—the wretch!—as if my life were not worth more than his! Let me come across him, that is all! Well, Lord King, you would have lost your right hand but that I looked from a covert among the ruins, and saw these men issue forth, stop one and another and let them go; so said I—'Ware wight, the wolf watches.' Then I took a bit of charcoal from my pocket, and on a wall where I knew Rhys would look, I drew a hammer, that is me; then an arrow in the air, and under it wavy lines, to signify swift flight over the water; and beyond that two cups, to show that we would drink together again. I hope he will understand that, or he may despair for the loss of me."

"You say that you have agreed on signals by which to communicate."

"Well, Lord King, it is like this: I drove a rusty nail between two stones below the parapet, in a place not likely to be noticed, and when Rhys is summoned for the postern guard, he hangs a rope to the nail—single if it is for to-night, double for to-morrow night. When he is on guard there is no difficulty in getting in." And Smith imitated with his hand the action of one drinking.

"Would it be possible to get a strong party in that way?" Ælle asked.

Smith shook his head. Laelius was too vigilant for that.

"Well, look to my arms. The spike on the boss of my shield is loose, and every thing has got out of order since you have been away."

Smith was by no means grieved to hear such a testimony to his indispensable merits, but was not puffed up by praise, as a modest man might very possibly have been.

Æscwine sat in the great hall of the Gesithas, at Wlencing. Before him was a long table with benches to the right, to the left, and in front, on which the assistants sat. Heaps of wooden tallies strewed the table, each heap differing in colour according to the district it represented; and piles of silver and copper money lay on the other side, which men counted into leathern bags, and sealed each bag with a leaden seal.

It was the payment of the king's dues, and Æscwine was receiving those which were tendered in coin. As each sum was counted and acknowledged to be correct, he took the tally on which the account was scored and, splitting it lengthwise, gave half to him who paid, and kept the other for the king. It was impossible under such a system to keep long accounts. The impecunious debtor had to pay double at the next collection, and in case of failure was sold for a slave. But the right of sale was seldom enforced. Either the man's friends and the members of his gyld and his frank-pledge fellows made up the sum, or the king forgave the debt. Men were too scarce and useful to be hardly dealt with, and free Saxons were rarely sold in Ælle's day, unless hopelessly bad. The tythings looked after their own people, and most of the dues were from the corporate body rather than from the individual. The least part of the dues was paid in coin; féoh* meant cattle; and oxen, sheep, and farm produce, formed the bulk of the revenue. These payments in kind were not brought from all parts to Wlencing, they were sent to the nearest estate of the king, and received there by his reeve. Wlencing, however, was the centre of a district of its own, including the valley of the Adur, and its meadows were thronged with kine and sheep, its wharves with grain, pulse, and other matters, for the supply of the army which lay before Anderida.

Much of the business was done, though it was still early in the day, when word was brought from the ferry that a messenger had arrived with an order from the king. To save time, the runner cried across the river that every man who could bear arms was to join Ælle with all speed, and immediately some started to tell Æscwine, while others ran to warn the Marks up the river as far as the Stæningas, and a trysting hill was named toward which all should converge.

* Féoh, cattle, money—pecus, pecunia.

Æscwine and the ten Gesithas with him worked heartily, knowing that some emergency must have caused the sudden summons. One mustered the permanent garrison of the place which guarded the king's treasury, another rode westaway, warning Tarringas, Ferringas, Goringas, and the children of Pol, otherwise Bældæg. Then wheeling round he returned, and pushed his horse against the flanks of Cissa's hill till he came to the last steep slope, where he picketed his horse and hastened up on foot. He entered the great enclosure, sixty acres in extent, and looking round on the magnificent prospect, chose a spot on the south-western rampart from which he thought his signal would be most effective. He brought to this place materials for a fire, which were always in readiness up there—straw, dry logs, and green branches to make a smoke in the day time. The wind was too fresh at that height for his match to light, so he took shelter in a round pit near at hand, and soon kindled his torch of twisted straw, scrambled out and set fire to the beacon.

It quickly blazed up in the strong breeze, and the streaming smoke was seen far and wide. Men gathered together and sent out to inquire where they should muster, and the word was passed that all were to make for Wlencing.

Æscwine himself took a bag of the king's small coin and went to the strand, where a number of trading ships lay in the mud. A few only were from Saxon ports, most of them came from beyond the sea—from Armorica, from the mouth of the Sequana, from the ports of the Morini and from Friesland.

Some wanted to sell their merchandise, fill up their vessels with bales of wool, and be gone. But the kindly men of Friesland, who loved fighting as well as trading, were nowise loth to help their cousins. A sceat a day for each man as present pay, and contingent plunder, allured two hundred and twenty of them. The skippers had ten sceats each, thirty of which make a shilling.

With these, the garrison, and the men who

came in from the adjacent Marks, about four hundred and fifty in all, Æscwine marched two hours after noon. From Stæninga-Mark all down the river, parties of men were crossing that afternoon with their arms and provisions, and it began to be whispered with bated breath, that the Pendragon was coming to the relief of the great fortress with twenty thousand men, of whom four thousand were horsemen in complete armour, even the chests and foreheads of the chargers being guarded by plates of steel. Æscwine tried in vain either to contradict this rumour or to trace it to its source, it seemed to be in the air without any one being able to say whence it came. The shepherds on the hills, when they saw the marching men, slew each a sheep, and while the carcase was being dressed, sent for his arms. Then, leaving the flock to the boys and dogs, he flung the meat upon his shoulders and went to join the host. Women harnessed oxen to lumbering wains and, seated among their farm produce, with a slave to each yoke, left their homes among the downs for the camp where their people were gathering.

The trysting hill was a conical beacon, about two and a half miles from the sea, with a square camp of old days on its summit. Two hundred and fifty men met Æscwine here; and while he tarried for other parties who could be seen approaching, another runner arrived from Ælle, with orders to cross the fords of Ouse and encamp at Glyn, on the western side of the hill. Here another messenger would find them, and bring word of the place and time for meeting the king in the morning. To anxious inquiries concerning the Pendragon or, as the Saxons called him, the Bretwalda, the runner replied, it had been guessed by some that it was Ambrosius himself who was advancing against them; but that Cissa the Ætheling had discovered that it was Emyr of Calleva with less than six thousand men. He also stated that, from the number of boats he had secretly collected in the creeks, it was conjectured that Ælle intended to cross the water by night, and give battle to Emyr before the men of Anderida could come to his assistance.

Æscwine having heard this, set forward toward the Ouse with about seven hundred and fifty men. At the fords he chose three well-mounted Gesithas and rode with them up by the combes in which the battle was fought, to the encampment which overlooked them. Many of the dead had been dragged from their shallow graves by the wolf, and torn by the hill fox; ravens and carrion crows flapped along near the ground with guttural cry, and the air was heavy with fetid gusts until the top was gained where the sea breeze blew. They looked from the height to the spot on which their handful of people moved like ants, and the long train of waggons trailed far behind. They gazed down the valley to the sea, where six years before the tide ran red at Mercredesburne. Far away to the eastward a thin blue cloud hung over the towers of Anderida, but they discerned no movement of human life. Then they rode round the curving crest of the hill, looking sharply for signs of friend or foe, but none could they see, save the wild bees which dashed angrily at the intruders with threatening hum.

They were turning away with a last glance over the forest, when from a bare knoll, some two leagues away, came a sudden flash.

"What can that be?" all four exclaimed in a breath.

"It can be nothing else than the flash of armour," Æscwine said after a pause. "But who can it be, and why there, out of the track of our people or of any enemy, unless indeed they are coming hither?"

One of the Gesithas descended as quickly as was consistent with safety to hasten the slow waggons, and to bid the runner from the Saxon camp go up to Æscwine who, with the two other Gesithas, kept watch on the hill. It wanted a full hour to sunset, but the high trees intercepted the rays. At length, in an open space on the farther bank of the Ouse, where the long shadows did not reach, they saw a multitudinous twinkling which passed without break.

"Heavy-armed men in column," Æscwine said. "Try to estimate their number by the time they take to pass that space. Here comes the runner."

The man came up with an easy, springy step, and his deep chest, when he reached the top, scarcely heaved more rapidly than it did at the foot.

"Point out to me," Æscwine said, "the spot where you suppose Ælle will meet the Count of Calleva in the morning."

"Not on this river," the runner answered, indicating the Ouse; "the king would most likely catch the Britons as they cross that river on your right; you can see a bend of it yonder, may be six leagues off."

"So then if I were to bid you give a message to Ælle the King at sunrise to-morrow, you would seek him in that quarter."

"In that quarter, as you rightly say, unless fresh news came."

"Now look yonder. How many do you suppose have passed, Brorda?"

"If they are four abreast," the Gesith replied, "rather more than two thousand, but I am not sure that they are four abreast."

After looking for a short time the runner said—

"They are four abreast on the whole, though not very regular."

Now these runners were as remarkable for keen sight and close observation as for speed and endurance. In carrying messages over naked down or through trackless forest, the speedy foot would often be distanced by the heedful eye choosing the shortest or the easiest way. They would, if possible, get a view of their destination from some height, then mentally noting the lie of the ground, the course of the streams, the position of the sun, the direction of wind and clouds, together with numberless indications — the fruits of careful watching—they would go almost as straight as the homing bird.

Consequently much reliance was placed on their judgment of such matters as came within the range of their experience.

"In how few hours," Æscwine asked, "can you give my message?"

"To the king? Three hours the shortest way, two and a half keeping on the hard ground, rather more if the British horse are out."

"Say to Ælle that I have nine hundred men with me, and that I shall stay these strangers by wit and force as long as I can. I shall make a stand at the fords, and if driven back take refuge on this hill."

The runner was gone like a spirit. He deviated a little from his course to pick up a piece of board, a relic of one of the machines, which, when he came to the steepest part of the hill he sat upon, and guiding himself with an occasional touch of either foot, went down at a prodigious rate.

Æscwine and his companions took counsel together as they descended with more deliberation, and agreed that the waggons, of which there were between two and three score, might be made useful in defending the passage, if arranged so as to form a continuous barrier.

To gain time for his preparations, Æscwine sent three hundred of his best men up the right bank of the river, to harass and delay the advancing column. These fell on a British village at the narrowest part of the pass between the hills. It had suffered in the war and was almost deserted. Of the inhabitants who remained, some were slain, some fled toward the men of Calleva, carrying exaggerated reports of the Saxon strength.

It was an hour after sunset when the Britons made a serious attempt to gain the village, the defenders of which, finding themselves likely to be surrounded, set fire to it in many places and departed. The burning dwellings barred the road, and compelled the Britons to make a circuit; moreover, they had to move with caution, not knowing what was before them.

Emyr had left two thousand forest men

and a few hundreds of his heavy troops to decoy the Saxon King into the deep woods; while he himself, marching round with three thousand, effected his junction with Julius, and the two interposed with ten thousand men between Ælle and his camp, his fleet, his supplies, and forced him to fight where they pleased.

This scheme of Julius was in danger of being frustrated, unless Ælle was already so far on his way northward as to miss his runner.

Æscwine, meanwhile, had not wasted time. His Frisian sailors did wonders. Strong, patient, ingenious, no difficulty baffled them. The waggons were arranged in an irregular curve, in the centre of which was a scrubby island which separated the upper from the nether fords, while the extremities of the line rested on dangerous swamps. The waggons were about a fathom apart, fastened together by the poles, and under the poles young trees were lashed, with their branches spreading toward the enemy, and their butts fixed in the mud. At the upper end of the line, faggots were fastened under the axle-trees, which to some extent turned the current and deepened the river's bed; while at the shallower parts the rank was doubled, and impediments placed to trip up an enemy.

It was rather dark when Emyr reached the fords, and ordered an immediate attack. It was of great importance that his junction with Julius should not be delayed, and he suspected the enemy before him was weak —he did not know how weak. Under cover of the archers and slingers on the bank, the Britons entered the water, hurling their javelins against the waggons. The missiles did but little harm in the obscurity, and the warriors, slipping and stumbling, advanced in a rather disorderly fashion within reach of the Saxon sword. They pressed on gallantly, and finding they were wasting their strength fighting in the water, threw their shields over their heads, and scrambled into the waggons. As fast as one was killed or thrown back, others thrust themselves up, and in one place the first line was carried. Shouts of triumph brought fresh assailants to the spot, who leaped into the water between the lines, where they fell by scores. In the gloom men could scarcely see where to strike. Æscwine had his hands full in another part of the battle, and Brorda, with a reserve of two hundred men on the left bank, ascertained, with difficulty, whereabouts his help was needed; while the Count of Calleva, slowly finding out the state of the struggle, desisted from his other attacks, and threw his full weight upon the enemy's weak point. The second barrier was forced, and only Brorda and his little phalanx stood between the shore and nearly three thousand men, who came rushing like a flood through the opening in the Saxon line. The locked shields were forced back but held their formation, and the Saxons from the waggons rallied on the bank behind them. The moon between light clouds, shone with sufficient clearness to enable Æscwine to discover the posture of affairs. The nether ford was abandoned by the Britons, who could be distinguished as they ran up the bank. The men below and those on the island were got together, formed a wedge as well as the state of the case would allow, and pushed strongly up stream. They were only five hundred, but they thrust aside the men of Calleva, and took some of the pressure off Brorda's band. Again the Britons thronged around, elated by success. Half a dozen hands grasped the upper edge of a shield, dragging it down, while as many sharp-pointed, double-edged Roman swords sought for weak points in the harness. Like a bull at bay before the wolves, each stout Saxon and burly Frisian exacted more than life for life, but the odds were heavy against them. Midnight was passed, the moon went on her journey from one thin cloud to another, careless of wounds or weariness. Sword and shield grew heavy, and the strong arm ached though the heart was steadfast. Æscwine's shout was heard, "Close up, close up!" and from Brorda, as answer, "Keep cool, and strike straight!" The Gesithas had promised to stay the enemy, and they would do it —they had done it.

Shrill cries from the rear pierced through the noise of the battle, and the words "Cissa the Ætheling," could be distinguished. The women from their place of safety had heard the sounds by which the succours from Ælle warned their countrymen that help was at hand, and hastened to cheer their hard-pressed friends.

Cissa soon came up with fifteen hundred men, and after a short, fierce struggle, drove the Britons back.

Darkness and fatigue put an end to the combat, and each party encamped by the river-side.

CHAPTER V.

ÆLLE crossed the water in his boats by starlight, and marched in such a direction as would enable Cissa to join him readily. He guessed that as soon as Julius was informed of the events of the night, he would send to the Ouse all the bands not required to garrison the city, and endeavour to crush the Saxon detachment. He thought that, possibly, these bands might be hurried forward in scattering fashion, which would give an opportunity of inflicting on them heavy punishment.

Cissa, with his comparatively fresh troops, worked through the night, while Æscwine's men slept. Oxen were harnessed to the wains at the nether ford, which drew them out of the water and brought them up to the scene of strife. Some waggons were in like manner got out of the upper ford. Then, with the earliest grey of dawn, the wounded were sought out and placed in the wains, women went with them to bind up their hurts, and to supply them with water; the train set off toward the spot where Ælle had appointed to meet them, and arrived without mischance.

The British sentinels heard the creaking of the unwieldy vehicles, but the darkness prevented any discovery of what was going on. Emyr had sent messengers to hasten forward the force left in the forest, and awaited their arrival to renew the attack. He despatched men to Julius with tidings of what had occurred, and hoped that a strong detachment from Anderida would fall on the Saxon rear in the heat of the conflict. While his men were breaking their fast, news reached the Count of Calleva that the Saxons were gone; before he could get his people fairly on the track precious time had been lost. Instead

ANDERIDA.

of the Saxon rearguard, he met Farinmail's cavalry.

Farinmail, as soon as he heard the statement of the messenger, set out with his five hundred horsemen, each carrying an archer behind him. He had the wit to see that the Saxons would not stay at the fords to be cracked like nuts, and he made all haste along the Roman road, hoping to catch them on their retreat, to harass, embarrass, and impede them till Emyr and Julius came up. As he crossed the bridge over the Cuckmare, it occurred to him that such an important point should have a strong guard, but he doubted not that Julius or some one would see to it. He kept to the road and missed the Saxons, who went farther north.

Ælle had drawn out his whole strength, which amounted, with Æscwine's reinforcement, to more than six thousand men. Of these he sent two thousand to guard the bridge over the Cuckmare by which Farinmail had passed, and the rest he concealed among the wooded hills a little to the north of the Roman road. His dispositions were hardly completed, when Farinmail's infantry were seen issuing from their fortified camp, and following in the track of their leader. Ælle immediately despatched two thousand men, most of them sailors, headed by Cymen, to surprise this camp, and so to close the road from Anderida to the fords. The detachment was screened by the nature of the ground, and seized the camp, which was almost deserted, without the slightest difficulty.

Farinmail's infantry marched swiftly along the well-paved road, and were comforted by the sight of another column of foot about a mile behind them, which they supposed to be the main body from Anderida. They were nearly an hour from their camp, when the scouts came in with a report that the bridge over the Cuckmare was occupied by a small body of Saxons. The men of Gwent halted, and the leaders, having consulted what was to be done, resolved to clear the bridge.

Ælle now had his enemies effectually

divided into three parts. The Count of Calleva and Farinmail were near the fords, while Cissa was breaking down the bridge between them and the city, as he had previously cut the one higher up, by which he had retreated earlier in the day. The men of Gwent were in a trap in the middle; and Julius was crossing the long bridge with three thousand soldiers, to find his way barred by the fortified camp he had so carefully constructed.

The men of Gwent attempted to carry the bridge with a rush, but met with solid resistance from an enemy more numerous than the scouts had reported. Saxons rose up from unexpected lurking places, and assailed the column on either flank, throwing it into confusion; while the troops in the rear, supposed to be Julius, proved to be Ælle. Hemmed in on all sides by a foe who offered no quarter, they fell in their ranks, selling their lives dearly.

Julius left the city guard and a hundred or so besides, under Laelius, to protect the place from surprise. He started nearly an hour later than the men of Gwent, and having passed the fortified bridge-head, marched along the Roman road which traversed Farinmail's camp. He neglected none of the regular precautions on the march, but observed them rather as a matter of formal discipline than as anticipating danger so near home. His vanguard, entering the camp before them, were not a little scandalized to find the gates open and no one on duty either there or anywhere else, so far as could be seen. As soon as they were fairly inside, men rose from ambush, and shut the gates ; while the concealed Saxons, issuing forth, cut the unlucky advanced guard to pieces. The Britons behind them supposed that there was treachery on the part of the men of Gwent, but were undeceived by the Saxons, who showed themselves on the rampart. There would have been a furious attack on the palisade, and unavailing slaughter ; but Julius held back his men, and ordered two beams to be brought and used as rams against the gates. The Saxons threw darts and stones from above, but the assailants, infuriated at the deception practised on them, heeded not the storm. The gates were smashed to splinters, and, rams in front, the men of Anderida forced their way into the camp. Vortipore, with his guard, was in the very van of the fight, determined to recover his old reputation for reckless valour. The unorganized sailors, however formidable man to man, were thrust back by the dense column pressing through the gate, headed by the veterans of Vortimer's victories, the best disciplined soldiers in Britain.

Julius took five hundred of those who had not as yet been able to enter, and moving swiftly round to the opposite side of the camp, found the gates there without watch or guard. While some were scrambling over to undo the bolts and bars, Julius, with Bael's help, mounted the rampart and got up to a wooden platform which commanded a good view of the straight Roman road. At the distance of a league was a column of foot, the form and movement of which, even so far away and shrouded in dust, were perceptibly unlike those of either Gwent or Calleva. A few moments' observation sufficed to show that of whatever tribe it might be, it was moving rapidly toward the camp.

"Those are not Britons," Julius said. "If they are Saxons———" and he stopped, trying to take in all the relations of the case. Bael said—

"They are Saxons. The men of Gwent are after the Saxons, and Ælle has been after the men of Gwent. It is a bad business."

"Bad indeed. If we are caught in here we shall not see the city again."

"You must get out of this," Bael remarked, "but how?"

"Trumpets on this side of the camp will be useless," Julius said. "We must charge down between these rows of booths, and cut our way."

"The wind is west. I will fire the booths behind you. When you come to the other side take the top of the rampart, and slay the fliers."

"Perhaps that is the best plan. Ælle cannot be here for twenty minutes."

So Julius, dividing his men into two bodies, charged headlong into the Saxon rear, and drove the enemies right and left, just in time to save Vortipore, who was rather too fat for long-continued efforts. He was beginning to breathe short and strike wild when he met Cymen, for whom he would have been no match in his best days. His sword glanced on the boss of the Ætheling's shield. Cymen's first blow beat down his adversary's guard, and the second cleft his helmet. The battle was hot over the body, when Julius came to the rescue, and the palace guard carried away their master. The flames, kindled in many places by Bael, leaped swiftly from booth to booth till the width of the camp was burning. The Britons on the rampart were safe, and held together, but the Saxons, nearer to the fire and blinded by the smoke, rushed madly hither and thither, and lost many of their number. At length the trumpets sounded a retreat, when there was not too much time to spare, for Ælle was close to the other side of the camp before the British rearguard was a furlong away.

The Saxons overtook the rearguard, which fell back skirmishing, and suffering severely. Julius meantime had sent for Laelius and every fighting man from the city, feeling assured that Ælle was before him, and that Anderida would not be assaulted on the other side for the present. It was obvious that the army could not avoid a battle, as it was impossible to get it inside the gates while the Saxons were hanging on its rear. He wished to fight in such a position that the engines on the fortification of the bridge-head might be brought to bear upon the enemy; but the rearguard was so cut up that there was some fear of its giving way, an event which would be dangerous if it should occur before he were settled in his position.

The men of Anderida were drawn up in six divisions of about five hundred men each, on a rising ground three furlongs from the bridge-head. Three of the divisions formed the front line and three were in reserve, the wings being at an obtuse angle with the centre, so as to command the lower ground and the road which crossed it.

The Saxons were not in their usual compact order. In the eager chase they were scattered, skirmishing on the road and on either side of it. The running fight which the Britons were sustaining, was not suitable to their genius. They love forward movements, and it was a welcome sound when the shrill trumpets bade them seek shelter between the openings of the front line. The long loose array of the pursuers was met half-way up the slope by a charge of heavy-armed troops, disciplined in the Roman fashion, which took them in front and on both flanks. They were borne down, broken up into small groups, most of which were cut to pieces where they stood, and there was great slaughter. Thorsten the tall, happily unembarrassed by drink, made a gallant stand with threescore of his Scandinavians, whose long axes rose and fell like threshers' flails. Ent rushed valiantly enough upon Bael till he was within a yard of his enemy, when a sudden horror seized him, and he turned and fled. A kick from Bael's misshapen foot sent him high in the air, where he turned over once or twice, and fell like a frog into a weedy pool.

Ælle was in the rear, having been detained by the necessity of collecting and encouraging the stragglers of Cymen's broken band. Many were cowed by the disaster which had befallen them, more than five hundred of their number having perished in the camp. Some fell by the sword in their straggling attempts to escape, some were smothered in the smoke, and all the badly wounded were burnt. The Saxon King stood on the scorched rampart, and swore by the one-handed War-god, that as the men of Anderida had done to his, so he would do to them when the time came.

Eormenred and his fellows were among those who escaped from the camp. Driven back among the huts by the charge of Julius they were separated from each other in the surging crowd. Eormenred, faithfully helped by Bosa and the other Beorlafingas, forced a way through the throng looking everywhere for his son Eostrewine. They reached the foot of the rampart and were about to return, when Esné, scorched and black, emerged from the smoke with the lad on his back. They were not recognised till the outlaw called to Eormenred asking if he had any drink for his son. Eormenred and Bosa had enough water in their bottles to give the boy a draught and to wash his face, whereupon he revived speedily. He had been thrown down in the confusion and trampled on. Just then a great rush was made at the vallum on that side, Cymen leading the way. Here it was that the main body of the Saxons broke through. They swept aside the Britons, tore up the stakes which they threw into the foss, and slid down safely. Esné would have taken Eostrewine on his back again, but the youngster would not hear of it, declaring himself quite capable of taking his own part, so they put him in the midst of them.

Ælle now came up with two thousand and seven hundred warriors in close order, to restore the fortune of the day. It was quite time he should come. Osmund and his Jutes were broken and overpowered in the centre. On the right Thorsten's axe-men were dropping fast, for Julius had sent a party against them with spear and pilum. As the Scandinavians raised their two-handed weapons for a blow, they were thrust through with the lance or the heavy dart. On the left Ceolwulf held his men together, but the green hillside was dotted with Saxon corpses. As Ælle advanced, the Britons fell back to their first position, and as he came nearer, passed through the intervals of the rear divisons, which in their turn retired in the same manner as the Saxons continued their approach. So they passed over the summit of the rising ground, and for some distance down the opposite slope. Seeing the open order the foe had assumed, and also that the bridgehead was close at hand, Ælle resolved to charge and drive the Britons into the marshes. He gave the word, but the solid mass was heavy to move, and the feet did not go together; most of them belonged to seafarers unapt to terrestrial movements. By degrees it got into a lumbering trot, with a terrible rattling of shields, and harness clattering to the irregular motion. The phalanx bore down on the enemy, gradually increasing its pace; but the Britons opened to the right and left, and before the unwieldy body could be checked, it was within twenty fathoms of the bridge-head, on whose towers catapult and balista twanged and clanged, sending darts and stones into the thick ranks. The men of Anderida charged on both flanks, and increased the difficulty the Saxons experienced in getting their heads the other way. They would gladly have assailed the fortification, and Julius hoped they would do so, but Ælle knew better than to venture on such a step without the slightest preparation, and giving the signal to retreat, fought his way out of reach of the enemy's shot. It was by this time two hours after noon, and while the men sat on the grass eating the food they had brought with them, each having meat for three days, the king considered within himself what it were best to do. He had slain the men of Gwent, fifteen hundred in number, and cut off Anderida from her allies, but his own losses in the course of the day were not far short of a thousand men, while Julius had suffered to perhaps a third of that extent, and had carried off his wounded.

Cissa sent word that he had broken down all the bridges, but he doubted whether he could prevent Emyr and Farinmail from crossing, as they were so strong in archers, who shot at the Saxons while the other Britons prepared a raft to cross. He could not prevent their getting over in the night, and desired to know his father's wishes.

Ælle sent word to his son that he was by no means to risk a battle, but to watch the enemy closely, and to give warning of all his moves.

Then the king thought that it would be a good thing if he could catch his enemies as they crossed the river, and cripple them so that Cissa might hold them at bay with two thousand men. But it would be no easy task to execute this plan without exposing himself to a counter blow from Julius, whom he feared more than all his other adversaries combined. Effectually to carry out his design it would be needful to leave before the fort a force strong enough to repel any attack from the city, or at least to prevent Julius sending help to his allies while Ælle was crushing them. Cymen, with eleven hundred men, could be spared for this duty, but it was a great risk, and the young man received much good counsel from his father, with strict injunctions to be drawn by no means from his defensive position.

Four hours after noon a messenger came

from Cissa with tidings that the British horse had gone up the river, and that a magic raft, carrying two hundred men, crossed and recrossed without help from human hands; while crowds of archers made it impossible for a Saxon to show himself within a hundred yards without a wound, no armour being proof against the Welsh shafts at that distance.

As to the magic raft, it was the work of a cunning man of Calleva. He chose a suitable spot on a bend of the stream, where a small water-course on the opposite side had produced a shoal convenient for a landing place. Then on the curving shore which looked down a reach of the river, he drove in a post to which was attached a long rope which would reach from the post to the place from which the raft was to start, and also to the shoal where it was destined to arrive. The rope was made fast to the raft, in such a way as to hold it at a certain angle with the stream, when the weight of the current pushed it across. The raft was set at the contrary angle when it was desired to go the other way. It took about ten minutes to go and return to the point whence it had set out.

Ælle sent back word that Cissa was not to hinder the crossing, and that the king would come to his aid without delay. Accordingly two thousand of the freshest of the Saxons marched at once, and reached the river by the time eighteen hundred of Emyr's heavy-armed men were drawn up on the Saxon shore. Leaving three hundred to oppose the horsemen at the only place where it seemed possible that they should cross the smaller stream, he drew up his own men with Cissa's in the usual triangular form, and moved against the spearmen of Calleva, who advanced to meet them in a solid parallelogram, with a front of two hundred men, each raft load forming a fresh rank in the rear.

The two masses hurtled together with shouts and crashing of spear-shafts. The point of the triangle, where the biggest and boldest men stood, sank deeply into the ranks of the spearmen. Thrust on by those behind, they were forced through to the other side with scarcely a chance of striking a blow, except with their shield-bosses. The wider part of the wedge followed, crushing and trampling all before it. Men were forced down, standards were overthrown, the two parts of the divided parallelogram were driven farther and farther apart in confused heaps. Then the triangle opening out enclosed Emyr's men between itself and the river. Fresh troops coming over during the heat of the conflict increased the tumult, but added nothing to the Count's strength. Emyr fell in the hottest of the fight, and the battle became mere slaughter, for not one of his chiefs turned back from the enemy. Some of the men cast away their arms and swam across the river; some crawled between the bushes and through the little rivulet to Farinmail; but of two thousand four hundred who came over before the battle was done, a bare two hundred went back. Never again did bard sing the deeds of the dauntless Spears of Calleva.

Farinmail, embarrassed by thickets and bogs almost impassable for horse, was late in reaching his destination. His guides, however, brought him to the ford while the desperate struggle was still raging. He heard the shout of battle and the ringing of steel; he saw the maddened broil of furious hosts, the slayers and the slain. One headlong charge of his gallant troopers might yet turn the scales, and redeem the day for Britain; but the charge was never made. All along the ford felled trees presented their branchlets to the impatient horsemen, who rushed their chargers at the barrier and hacked at the twigs with keen broadswords, but all in vain. A wall of stone and lime would not have stayed them more absolutely. Farinmail came out of the water and rode up and down the bank to seek another passage. In one direction a deep morass, in another steep banks stopped him, and the little stream which formed the shoal where the raft landed its passengers, now protected the flank of the Saxons. Meantime the battle was going against his friends. He struck down the guide who told him that there was no other crossing place for miles, and wheeling in a wide circuit, put his horse at top speed at the brook. The good steed did his best, but the jump was too wide; he got his fore feet on to the other bank, and after a desperate scramble fell back into the water. Farinmail was under him, and was insensible when rescued.

The battle on the other shore was done. The horsemen retreated slowly and with heavy hearts, bearing their injured captain in a litter made of cloaks fastened on two straight saplings.

CHAPTER VI.

VORTIPORE lay in a large room on the first floor of the palace, with windows open on both sides for the sake of coolness. On disarming him it was discovered that besides the severe cut on the head, he had received other injuries when he was down in the press.

Bronwen stood by his couch cooling him, and driving away the flies with a fan of feathers, or giving him whey, slightly acidulated, from a jar wrapped about with wet cloths. A tall bronze lamp, so placed as not to throw the light in his eyes, made a radiance in the centre of the apartment, leaving the corners in obscurity. Out of the gloom came silvery flashes, and a trilling stream of harp-notes suggesting freshness and coolness, like the tinkling dropping of water into a cavern lake.

Vortipore's hand soon began beating time to the strain with feeble joy, and Bronwen's long-handled fan waved to the rhythm. Then a voice blended with the prelude, in notes where art concealed in some degree the waning powers of age. Perhaps a younger throat might have pleased the girl, but to Vortipore's ear Howel Hên was ever young as he sang—

> " Morning pale the earth renews,
> Flowery buds and bells diffuse
> Fragrance to the early dews.
>
> " Where reflected shapes befool
> Heedless eyes, are willows cool,
> Dripping in the pearly pool.
>
> " From the pool a streamlet strays,
> Wandering under burning rays,
> Gelid in the thirsty ways.
>
> " Till from rock with plumes of fern
> Shivering, fleecily falls the burn,
> And the drops to drops return.

"Cooling to the cooling skies
See the rainbow dew-dust flies,
Till dun wings of eve arise."

Then, changing his style, he sang to a slumberous tune—

"On dull wing comes evening still,
Pallid stars the twilight fill,
Creeping o'er the lonely hill.

"From the hill-fold dusk and grey,
Solitary, far away,
Faintly sounds the watch-dog's bay.

"From the dim, the drowsy shore
Floats the breakers' sudden roar,
Ceasing, makes the stillness more.

"Sleep the birds in thick-leaved trees,
O'er the forest sleeps the breeze,
Over heaving summer seas."

The hand had moved slowly and more slowly till it lay still, and the old man saw that Vortipore was sleeping. He struck a few deep chords which ran into a flowing cadence, swelling and dying away again into silence. Then he came from his corner and stood with Bronwen behind the couch, watching the face which twitched from pain.

"Is there any danger?" the girl asked. "Will he soon recover?"

"He will not rise from this couch," the old man said, as if to himself, "but he will live as long as you, or I, or any of us."

"What do you mean? Have you really seen the fatal vision?"

"I have seen enough. One hour will close the eyes of every one within these walls. You may escape, if you will—you and another."

"I do not believe you have seen the vision," Bronwen muttered. "If there were anything in it you would take care of yourself."

"Take care of myself," Howel Hên repeated, in a tone which startled the girl, low as it was. "Did you never hear how the ravens refuse to quit their nest in the old tree when it is being cut and nods to its fall?"

But the murmuring voices disturbed the wounded man, who began to stir uneasily, and the harper went back to his seat and sang—

"Deep within the hoary wood,
A thousand years the oak has stood
Where the ravens rear their brood.

"Ere the hoary forest grew,
When the earth was bare and new,
O'er the land a raven flew.

"Prying wheeled the raven then,
Croaked and turned his head again,
Dropped an acorn in the fen.

"Grew the oak in shine and shade,
Woodlands flourished and decayed,
Forest upon forest laid.

"So from out the humid meres
The slow land itself uprears
Higher every thousand years.

"Ever in the midmost space
Built the birds of ancient race
Their ancestral dwelling-place.

"Came the fellers to the wood
Where the raven's dwelling stood,
Hewing, hewing, where they would.

"Hewing, hewing, stroke on stroke,
At the venerable oak,
Where the lineal ravens croak.

"Shook the giant to his fall,
  Limbs and branches quivered all
  With a thrill funereal.

"Said the ravens, 'Shall we fly
  Other realms to amplify?
  Better in our own to die.'

"So the stem of old renown,
  With the ravens in its crown
  Dead, to earth came crashing down."

"That is not right," Vortipore said querulously. "You have altered it."

Bronwen raised her father's head and gave him drink, and at that moment the medicus entered with an assistant, and the bishop.

The medicus examined his patient, asked if his powers of speech, sight, and hearing were impaired, and expressed a hope that there was no fracture of the skull, as he at first had feared.

"Surely," said Bronwen, who hated the man because he seemed to give her father needless pain, "you must know whether it is so or not, after cutting and scraping as you did this morning."

"You must know, lady," replied the healer severely, "that a blow on one part of the head may cause a fracture in another, and also that there may be rupture within though the outer part be whole; and therefore, although the specillum——" and he held up an instrument like a large pointless pin, made of silver.

"Curse the specillum!" said Howel Hên. "The skull was not broken this morning, and it is not likely to have broken itself since."

"I will concede," answered the medicus with a wave of the hand, "that it is lawful to hope that the solidity of the skull resisted the stroke."

The assistant, meantime, had removed the bandages and laid bare the wound, and it was decided to substitute a simple dressing of linen steeped in vinegar, and over that wool, also moistened with vinegar, for the plaster of vine leaves, triturated in goose-grease, which had been removed. When his head was bound up again, Vortipore asked, in a feeble voice, if he could have some wine.

"Wine!—the last thing in the world; as well drink hemlock juice."

"I do not believe a little wine would do any harm," said Bronwen. "I do not mean mere wine, but mixed four or five to one."

"Lady, you must know that by an ancient law, a patient who took wine cóntrary to the order of the medicus, was put to death if he recovered. It was a good law, a very excellent law."

"In such a case," Howel Hên remarked, "a prudent man would have the physician murdered before he took to drinking."

"Or dispense with the services of the medicus altogether," the bishop added. "As well die of the disease as of the remedy. The epitaph runs, 'Morbus ad medicum, medicus ad mortem perduxit.'"

"If I am so great an evil," exclaimed the man of science with a rhetorical gesture, "why do you come to me? I do not flatter you while in health with fabled exploits of yourselves and your ancestors; nor on the other hand do I condemn you to eternal pains if you decline my ministrations in your last hours. You come to me hoping to be saved from the consequence of your evil passions. You quarrel, and your bodies are punctured or lacerated by ingenious instruments of destruction; or you are excruciated by diseases, the result of crapulence, ebriosity, luxury. Then you come on all-fours to the healer and behowl your conditions, exalting his skill and benignity. He administers hellebore to cure your madness, and perchance certain resinous substances for your other distempers. You die—the medicus has killed you. You recover—there was nothing amiss with you. We ask not for gratitude, but we do demand our modest recompense and honourable treatment."

"You forget the patient in the heat of your argument," said Bronwen.

"I will send a catapotium of mandragora, parsley seeds, and hyoscyamus, which you may give if he is restless, but not otherwise."

Therewith they all went away except Howel Hên, who lay in a corner of the room to see that the slaves tended his patron carefully and to solace him with music if he should wish for it. The bishop had promised to take his place on the ensuing night.

The medicus went to the house of Rhys, whom he had treated for the wound he received when his wife was carried off. But it was no longer in his capacity as a healer that he visited Rhys. He was drawn by a secret bond of sympathy, of which nothing was said between the men; in fact Rhys was scarcely aware of the existence of such a tie, and was quite ignorant of the nature and cause of it. Kynon the medicus concealed his intimacy with Rhys, always visiting his house at night, and going to it by stealthy, indirect ways. When he was roused from his bed to attend to Rhys' hurt, he was himself suffering from injuries inflicted by command of Prince Iorwerth, whose nose had been damaged by a stone, and who was dissatisfied with the progress of the cure. Though of low birth, Kynon was not of servile condition, as Iorwerth had falsely stated ; and being the only professor of the healing art in Anderida who had really studied medicine, his aid was invoked very generally, though often not till charms and other popular remedies had been tried and failed. He prided himself on the possession of, and the capacity to understand, an ancient codex of the eight books of Cornelius Celsus, and he often obtained rare drugs and hints as to their use from the ships trading to Anderida and neighbouring ports.

This man inquiring into the circumstances under which Rhys received his wound, had no difficulty in detecting the author of the injury, and indeed the very instruments. He even identified the club-man who struck down his friend, with a retainer of the prince who had been very active in annoying himself on a previous occasion, and had since died. As the wretch lay writhing in speechless agony, Kynon took an opportunity to inform him that the tortures he suffered were not due to his disease, but to a little pinch of something the medicus had taken the liberty of administering, and he warned his patient, that in that world whither he was going, he should be more respectful to scholars and men of science than he had, unhappily for himself, been in this. The sufferer made desperate efforts to reveal the secret, but the moment had been too well chosen, and the bravo expired, spending hopeless fury through his eyes. It was not love of cruelty which dictated this action, for the medicus would make great sacrifices to assuage the sufferings of his poorest patients, but the man was terribly vindictive.

As for Rhys, lamentably fallen away in flesh, he was greatly troubled at the absence of his friend Smith, whom he had relied on to take care of both when his own wits were wool-gathering.

Kynon had to some extent supplied the place left vacant by Smith, but not fully. He had no liking for the nightly explorations, and was wanting in physical massiveness, besides he refused to drink wine.

"Is there any news to-night?" Rhys inquired, when his friend came in.

"No. At least nothing since sunset, that has come to my ears."

"Have you seen or heard anything of Prince Iorwerth, of late?"

"Elidri came to me to-day, and said the Prince was ill; that if I would beg pardon for my ill behaviour the last time, I might be employed again."

"Elidri, that is his chamberlain. Well, what did you say?"

"I asked what was amiss with the most noble and virtuous Prince, and was informed that he had not been sober for a fortnight, and was haunted by spectres, larvæ. I said it was no case for me to take in hand; let him moderate his drinking, and send for a priest to lay the spectres in the Red Sea." At the recollection of which speech, Kynon laughed unpleasantly.

"Ah!" sighed Rhys, "I am sorry that was the end of the matter."

"It was not the end. The chamberlain then spoke frankly—implored me to come—to make my own conditions. 'I dare not return without you,' he said. 'I shall be whipped, tortured, I know not what. If he would once kill me, or'—and Elidri groaned—'if I dare kill myself.' And you expect me, said I, on mature consideration, again to put myself in the hands of this amiable youth. 'Listen,' said the chamberlain. 'Of course I knew there would be difficulties of this sort, and the Prince agreed to give a pledge—a hostage—what he holds dearest.' Not to weary you, I consented to that proposal; but I wonder—I wonder what the hostage will be?"

"Do not laugh in that way," Rhys said, "it reminds me of the creaking of the rack-rollers, when the men at the levers give a quarter turn."

"You are not the same man you were before—before that night; and indeed you cannot be the same. However, I thought, my friend Rhys takes an interest in all that pertains to the Prince, perhaps he would like to see the hostage. In fact, to deal openly, as friends should, I wish to leave her in your keeping while I go to the palace; for you are the only man whom I can trust not to give her up, either for force or fraud, till I return in safety."

"Keep *her*—give *her* up," Rhys repeated in bewildered tones.

"Yes, and you must swear to keep her truly, neither injuring her yourself nor permitting any other to injure her, unless I fail to return at the end of three hours. This you must swear on the Gospels, both to me and to the man who brings her. Are you ready to do this?"

"I am ready," Rhys replied, in a rough, constrained voice.

They went to the house of Kynon, where, in the atrium, two men with a covered litter awaited them, one of the twain being Elidri.

To him and to Kynon Rhys took the prescribed oath, and at the sound of his voice, a choked cry issued from the litter. Then Kynon went away with the chamberlain.

By this time, the cold light of early morning was streaming in at the compluvium, and Rhys, pulling aside the curtains of the litter, looked in. A beautiful woman, splendidly but meretriciously attired, lay there; her wrists and ankles bound with crimson silk, and a broken ivory wand in her mouth for a gag. Again a stifled cry gurgled in her throat, but Rhys heeded not. He looked at her for a short time with wooden face, then went away out of her sight to a corner where a water-clock was slowly filling its receptacle, drop by drop. The woman lay still, with large terrified eyes like a captured bird, starting at every little noise that broke the stillness, trembling for a few moments till the curtain rings of the litter rattled, then composing herself by a great effort again to listen, lest the horror should approach her unawares. At length, after several attempts, she raised herself so as to look over the side of the litter. She saw no one, nor any object of alarm, only from behind her came a measured dropping. Her panic terror increased to agony, and falling back, she struck her cheek against the side of the litter, so as partially to displace the ivory gag. Instantly the atrium rang with shriek upon shriek. "Kill me! Kill me at once! I cannot bear this! Oh, kill me!"

"Not yet," an austere voice replied; "the lower vessel is not full."

The screams were so piercing and incessant that, for fear of intrusion, Rhys replaced the gag in her mouth, and after this little attention she really seemed more comfortable.

Vortipore became restless from fever just before daylight, whereupon the catapotium was sought for that it might be administered. As, however, Howel Hên had given it to a dog, with a view to ascertain whether it were poisonous, the search was vain. Instead of mandragora and henbane, the bard soothed his patron with a song they two had made when Vortipore was courting the Damnonian Princess.

"A cuthan * coos in the lofty tree,
Cool the wind blows over the sea,
But my heart beats wearily.

"All the music of the air
Cannot win the ear of care,
When the heart beats wearily.

"By the level, blooming lea,
By broad river, wandering free,
Still my heart beats wearily.

"Fair, sweet flowers, but unknown,
Opulent country, not mine own,
Where the heart beats wearily.

"From a thymy, thin-aired hill
Sight and soul are straining still,
While my heart beats wearily.

"Strains to see, if but in dream,
Meadow, cot, and shining stream.
Whither my heart flies wearily.

"Where the brightest, dearest, best,
Turning soft eyes to the west,
Gazes, sighing wearily."

With the first strains of the harp, Vorti-

* Cuthan—wood-pigeon.

pore's thoughts flew from present pain back to the sunny morning, years ago, when southerly wind and swelling tide bore his ship up the broad estuary to the port of Isca.* Again he saw the red kine feeding in wide pastures, the swelling fields and woods, the white sails of corpulent merchantmen, and thought, what a nice country to have property in. He chuckled feebly as he recalled the solemn, dreary, ceremonious ride over the lands of his love, during the pauses of which he dedicated these lines to a more sprightly lady castaway.

The memory of this eastern flame evoked the image of her successor. One called up others—a motley throng, the figures growing hazier till they mingled in a dream.

* Exeter.

CHAPTER VII.

AFTER the heavy losses endured by the Britons there remained to them outside the walls of Anderida a thousand horsemen and archers of Gwent, eight hundred spearmen of Calleva, and two thousand foresters. All these recognized Farinmail as their chief, hoping soon to see him recover from the severe bruises he had received. But day after day passed, while the young chief seemed to get worse rather than better, and Comail continued to act in his name. Avoiding set battles, Comail beset the Saxons night and day, much to their annoyance.

Ælle had a strong position before the bridge-head, and Cissa lay to the west of him, interposed between the king and

Comail. The timber and brushwood, that might afford shelter to a lurking foe, had been cleared away for a considerable distance round both camps. All stakes having been removed from the channels, the fleet had access to the water surrounding the city, which was thus completely blockaded. The provision convoys were incessantly attacked, but a sufficiency of food found its way to the Saxon forces. Arrows armed with tow dipped in turpentine were shot among the booths, and when any caught fire, showers of forked shafts fell among the men who hastened to extinguish it. If a party turned out to chastise the insolent aggressors, Comail and his horsemen swooped down upon it, and sent it with diminished numbers home. But all this was of no real avail. While Ælle retained his position he held the city by the throat, and the combined efforts of the defenders failed to dislodge him.

The huge walls still held the assailant aloof, and the ample accumulation of provision set famine at defiance. Julius knew that the Saxon resources had been strained to the uttermost, and that when harvest time came, the bulk of Ælle's force must disperse to gather the crop. He reckoned on enjoying a reprieve during the month of September, and hoped, by that time at the farthest, to have aid from the Pendragon, and roll back the flood of Saxon encroachment. The indecisive battle of Mearcredes-burn had cost the Saxons so dearly, that for six years the Britons were left almost unmolested. Vortipore had wasted the interval of repose; but if such a breathing space were accorded to himself, what an army would he discipline; what fortresses he would rear of stone and lime, with noble engines on the walls. With sufficient cavalry, and a train of portable engines, he felt that he ought to be able to beat the unwieldy phalanx of the Saxons on any ground, and what could be done Julius would do. There was no doubt, at all events, that the city could hold out till September, and then, if no help came, he must do, as he had so often done before, without it.

Emyr the Count, and the chiefs who died with him, were buried by the river on whose brink they fell. Every solemn rite was duly performed, priests and relatives of the slain came from Calleva to pay the honours due to them. Psalms were sung and prayers recited as the sad procession wound its way to the graves, and encompassed the cairn reared in honour of the dead. Men lingered by the pile, and spoke despondingly of their city, which they compared to Britain when a tyrant drained her of her fighting men to support his own quarrel in Gaul. The warlike traditions of a people form no small portion of its strength. When few or none are left to gainsay the craven doctrine that men may part with freedom to save their goods; when the young are taught to think life more precious than honour and to disregard the brave old stories, the end is not far away. Conquest, or plundering invasion more cruel than settled conquest, is the doom of the nation unready with the sword. When intolerable oppression stings men at last to resistance, it is usually too late; the habits and instincts of the soldier cannot be revived, and their last state is worse than the first. With honour and courage all things are possible; without them we are the predestined slaves to the first tyrant or bully whom fortune may send across our path. A hundred years did not suffice to bridge the chasm made by the emigration under Maximus, and the expedition of Constantine.

"We lost then," said one speaker, "not only the sword and the hand that wielded it, but the spirit and discipline which made them formidable."

"More than that," murmured another, "with those men went the bond which held the tribes together. Since that time we have fallen asunder, stick from stick, like the unbound faggot."

"The priests tell us that it is the punishment due for our sins, yet they agree not either as to the fault, or how to amend it."

"A sheep can see the wolf," growled the first, "but it needs a dog, and a good one, to kill the enemy, or turn aside the apprehended danger."

So the old men talked by the graves of the chiefs, foreseeing the fate of their people.

Time passed away, amid sallies from the city and attacks of the forest Britons. The numbers and spirit of these last diminished as they found how little they prevailed. The spearmen of Calleva were summoned home to protect the city, where everything had fallen into disorder. It was now the twentieth day since Ælle's great success, and the beleaguered fortress was closely shut up. Occasional adventurers went and came under cover of darkness, but the boats of the Saxon fleet were not easily eluded. Adventurous Jutes and old Saxons, men of various races, driven from their home by chance of war, flocked continually to Ælle, hoping to repair their fortune. Æsc, King of the men of Kent, sent a thousand warriors to the assistance of his Saxon neighbour. All these elements of strength were welded by the force of Ælle's character into a homogeneous body of great power and tenacity.

Preparations for a grand assault upon Anderida were complete; the boats furnished with ladders were ready on the northern side, the fleet, similarly provided, was eager for a second attack on the southern face of the rampart. The question whether the entrenchment at the bridge-head should be stormed before the city itself was assailed, had been debated in a Witan of the whole army, and answered in the affirmative; but the time, the method, and all details connected with the enterprise were left to the king. He soon resolved that the attempt should be made some night when there was light enough for men to distinguish one from another, but not enough to enable the machines on the wall to take aim accurately. In the second place, the men must wear some mark not easily effaced, by which friends might be discerned from foes. In the third, he decided that squadrons of boats should threaten the bridge, both from above and from below, while the main push was made at the entrenchment. For several nights Ælle had roused the men at uncertain hours, assembled them silently, and marched them out as if for immediate action, only to dismiss them to their slumbers again, not without growling on their part.

Julius, to whom this exercise was related by his spies, had no difficulty in apprehending its significance. He redoubled his precautions, and arranged signals with his allies outside, to give them warning to fall on the rear of the Saxons in the crisis of the assault.

The fort at the bridge-head covered the whole of a piece of ground slightly elevated above the marsh, and joined to the higher land farther from the city by an isthmus cut through by the foss. The area of the fort was nearly an acre, its plan hexagonal, to suit the shape of the ground, and the ditch, twelve feet deep, was two-thirds full of water which soaked into it from above. The main road, thirty-two feet wide, ran straight through from side to side of the hexagon, the gate farthest from the bridge being flanked by two towers forty yards apart. The permanent garrison of four hundred and eighty men, was quartered in rows of huts running at right angles to the main road; but a second cohort now came from the city every night, and found shelter in booths made of branches placed along the foot of the rampart.

On the night of the twentieth day from the shutting up of the city, and the forty-fourth from Renatus' prophecy concerning the destruction thereof, Ælle sat with certain of his chiefs. There were the Æthelings, Cymen and Cissa; Osric the Ealdorman, who slew Ine the Ealdorman; Osmund the Jute, and Witgar, Captain of the men of Kent, sent by Æsc the King; and Thorsten the tall; Æscwine, Brorda, and Wyverth, Gesithas; and Wigmund, Ceolwulf, Eormenred, and Brihthelm. Each of these had his place and duty assigned to him. Osric the Ealdorman, and Osmund the Jute, and Thorsten, and Wigmund, were to assault the south-western tower, and Witgar, with the men of Kent, the north-western; while the king held his Gesithas, and fifteen hundred men in reserve at first. Ælle explained that by attacking the towers first, the machines of the enemy would be hindered from doing so much mischief. Cymen, with Ceolwulf, Eormenred, and Brihthelm, was to advance upon the bridge in boats, while Cissa protected the Saxons from the archers of Gwent and of the forest, and to do so more effectually was to come nearer to the city.

It was now near midnight. The signal for the assault on the towers would be four fires on the ridge between Ælle and Cissa. Men knew that the Britons communicated with each other by means of fires, and it was hoped that these would be confused with those.

Each man in this the earliest attack would wear a white cloth round his helmet as a distinguishing mark. Cymen was ordered not to move the boats till a further signal was made, and after these instructions he, with his subordinates, departed with the rest of the chiefs.

Ælle went through each division to see that it was duly prepared and provided with all things as he had ordered. Every man carried a faggot, and there were ladders, ropes, and chain hooks. Each faggot of the front rank was loosely connected by cords with those right and left, that they might not spread too much when others were thrown a-top of them, but tangle the rest together till they formed a mass on which men could cross. The fire-balls were invented by Smith, and consisted of handfuls of tow, dipped in pitch or grease, and enclosed in osier work, with strings attached, by means of which they could be slung over the heads of the combatants when lighted. The chain hooks were the ordinary grappling irons of the ships, which were to be thrown among the palisades and entangled there; then ropes being cast down to those below, men would clap on with a Yu—ho—yeoh—till part of the work came down.

Ælle, leaning with both hands on his sheathed sword, stood on the declivity which sloped to the fort. Beside him was the slave who bore his shield, and behind him a line of men stretched up the acclivity into darkness. He watched till the Pleiades rose clear in the sky, then raised his left arm to a horizontal position. The men in the rear imitated the gesture, and in a few seconds four fires began to spit and crackle on the ridge. Osric the Ealdorman, and Witgar of Kent came out of the obscurity on either side, and stood before the king.

" Hap helps the hardy," said Ælle, in a low but clear tone.

The two chiefs repeated the words, and departed from him as they came.

Then was heard, from right and left, a muffled sound as of many feet moving softly on the turf, and of dull contact of bodies, and a shifting of the shades of relative obscurity, like the changes perceptible in a field of corn when the breeze bends the rustling heads in a gloomy day of June.

Presently these signs passed away. Then from below came a quick challenge and a rush, whereupon sparks began to glow along the walls, which speedily burst into flames, throwing a wavering light on the water in the foss, and on a crowd of flashing, shifting figures on the wall and beneath it. Splash, splash, fell the faggots in lines together, short shrill shrieks rose up, and the Saxon battle cry was answered with shouts of "Hoi! Ynys Pridain!" Soon came the noises of closer conflict, and a breaking, tearing crash from the south-western corner, announced that the palisade there had given way. The lights glanced on helmets and swords, pushing up to the gap and falling back, the harsh jarring sound of the catapults became more frequent, until the assault slackened and came to a pause.

The attack was renewed after a short interval, and the appearances were repeated; but this time balls of fire were to be seen curving over from the outside into the interior of the fort. Ælle watched more intently, till a red glow was reflected by the smoke which arose from within; it spread, gaining in height and intensity, till the defenders of the wall were dark spots against the flame. Then he moved quickly down towards the main gate, having in front men carrying long planks, and next to them Smith, with a party of fellow-craftsmen provided with sledges, crows, and other tools wherewith to break the chains of the drawbridge.

Meantime the huts, made of dry boughs and tufts of grass, which rested against the inner slope of the rampart, burnt fiercely, scorching the Britons from the wall. Many of the bravest and the best were sacrificed in covering the retreat of those who ran round to the gate leading to the bridge. The south-westerly wind kept the seaward face tolerably clear, but on the other side to lee-ward, both Britons and Saxons perished from the smoke and heat. Ælle called off his men from the pursuit, not wishing to risk anything more until the fire had spent itself.

The retreating garrison, finding itself unpursued, began to tear up the floor of the bridge. It was no easy task, for the work was well fitted and fastened together, the old oak having hardened to the solidity of bronze, but at the same time losing its toughness and becoming splintery. With the help of tools and shears from the tower, they ripped off the planking for about forty yards, together with the side rails and the cross pieces, but the heavy longitudinal timbers from one set of piles to another were too massive to be either lifted or cut in a short time with the means at hand. The woodwork thus ripped off was so arranged as to form a parapet to the fragment of the bridge close to the new tower built by Julius, to which it formed an outwork, covering the gate with an openwork bastion, which projected twelve yards into the marsh.

The signal for the boats to attack the bridge was made at the same time that Ælle advanced against the gate of the fort, but owing to the rapid spread of the fire, and its efficacy in causing the evacuation of the bridge-head, they were still entangled among the booms anchored above and below, when the fighting concluded. The tide turned, and brought back on them all the floating spars they had cut adrift, the dawn was brightening the eastward sky, and the engines on the towers were beginning to send a morning greeting in a shower of darts and stones. Still the crews persevered, the increasing light helping them to overcome the intricate impediments to their progress, till a messenger arrived from the king with orders that they should desist.

The fire in the fort at the bridge-head had burnt itself out. In the middle space stood the remains of huts, long rows of clay walls standing with their feet in embers covered with a light white ash, from which coils of thin blue smoke went spiring up. All round the rampart was a line of similar destruction, from which ghastly forms protruded themselves in many places, especially at the north eastern part.

A number of Saxons had gone along the bridge to the spot where it was destroyed. There they stood looking at the tower, at the sedgy pools, and tufts of flags and rushes, where morning mists were creeping.

"Ugh!" one of them exclaimed, "one wants a horn of ale against the chill."

"You miss the good fire," said another, "where you singed your feathers no long while ago. You smell of burning even now."

Ent, who had been steadfastly regarding the tower before him, and the wood so carefully arranged on the remains of the bridge, said—

"I could show you the way to make a better bonfire than that." Then, as the men crowded round him, he continued, "You see the stack of firewood those Welshmen have piled, with openings everywhere to promote the draught. Yes. You see those planks sticking out of the mud below, as if they were intended to make a great fire—you do. Can none of you lubberly buffel-heads put that and that together? Well, thank the gods, there is plenty of fools' meat."

"Tell'ee what, ye miserable little manikin," said a strapping young fellow, "if ye were but half a size larger, I'd put this and this together, but one dares not touch ye, lest one should spoil ye."

So saying, he brought down his open hand on the giant's back with a force which sent the little man staggering forward, and he would have fallen into the mud below, but for another burly blockhead who caught him by the arm and swung him back on to the platform.

Ent rewarded his preserver with a furious kick on the shin, and was proceeding to extremities of language, when pulling off the cap which had been knocked over his eyes, he saw Ælle the King.

"Is there no place but this to play fools' tricks in? With the strengthening light you will have a flight of sweetmeats from up there, and I do not wish to lose you, though you might be wiser than you are."

"That is true, Lord King," cried Ent; "I was just telling them so."

"And pray what is your wisdom doing here?" Ælle inquired.

"He was telling us what a fine fire that stack of wood might furnish if we had only wit enough to set a light to it."

The king looked at the piles of plank, at the tower, and at Ent; then said—

"This bracelet to him who shows how to do it, and a hogshead of ale for those who help to accomplish it."

When the king left, Ent, quite restored to good humour, said—

"Now, silence all. Do not ask my pardon. I forgive you. You see the mist is thickening; our operations will be undiscovered if you can but be quiet. There are ropes which were used last night—fetch them. There are faggots, dry and wet—fetch them, but especially the dry. There are embers still burning—I must have a quantity of them; but how to carry them? I shall think of that."

The men departed from their instructor, silently enough, and the word was passed not to say anything of what was going on, for—

"We are quite enough to drink one hogshead of ale," they said.

Only one lingered. He laid his hand tenderly on Ent's shoulder—

"Dear lad, you might be killed, you know."

"I may," replied Ent, drawing himself up, "but what then? My brethren in arms will mourn for me, Ælle will miss me, all the——"

"Ay, dear lad, but if you are killed before the wood is kindled, we shall not get the hogshead of ale. Tell me your plan."

CHAPTER VIII.

Kynon returned in safety to his house before the time appointed had elapsed, and the hostage was taken back to the palace by Elidri and his fellow. Again, and a third time, with short intervals between, the covered litter stood in the atrium of the healer's dwelling, and Rhys kept his watch with immovable visage. The woman was becoming accustomed to the proceeding, and no longer expected the wall to open and disclose a fiend with scorpion whip, ready to scourge her to her doom.

The minutes stole away, Rhys began to be restless, the water was rising to the little lip; drop, drop, drop, each circle expanding to the circumference of the vessel, and quivering back with lovely intersecting curves. Rhys checked the restless feeling, the morsel was sweet in his mouth, why should he hasten to swallow it. Drop, drop, it is filling, full, brimming, the water stands above the lip, another drop—one more, and a tiny streamlet runs pattering into the pitcher below.

Then Rhys rose, and putting his hand inside his frock, drew from its sheath a thin, keen knife. The handle was black, cut in diamonds for surer gripe; the blade was shining black as clear winter ice; the shape was cruel, suggesting unhallowed carving of human limbs. It was a pet knife of Kynon's, and Rhys contemplated it fondly, as he stood by the litter, sharpening the long blade on the palm of his hand, and trying its edge on his nail.

As the woman followed every motion with white-ringed eyes, the cold hand seemed to be laid on her heart. From a neighbouring roof a clear voice came floating down.

and was answered by another farther away, singing—

> *First voice*—" The day is long, is long, sweetheart,
> Slow, slow the sun's decline."
>
> *Second voice*—" Ah, darkness comes apace, sweetheart,
> And darker fears are mine."
>
> *First voice*—" Night's starry curtain drawn, sweetheart,
> Gay love may laugh unseen."
>
> *Second voice*—" Ah, hate may watch with love, sweetheart,
> And death peer in between."

Some of the words were scarcely audible, but Rhys knew the song well. Five years ago he used to sing it on the terrace, watching for the lithe figure, indistinct in the summer twilight; listening for the tones which thrilled the warm air into sweetness. He thought of the kind old father, whose words came back with the song—

"I have spoiled her, Rhys, and you have spoiled her. When she angers you, remember that she is not alone to blame."

After a silent pause, which seemed long, he turned with a sigh, and a more human look on his face. "I cannot forgive now—for the old man's sake I cannot punish. For his sake repent, and come in my way no more."

With these words Rhys cut the bonds on his wife's ankles and wrists, and sheathing his knife, disappeared through the passage at the back of the atrium, closing the doors and fastening them with the bolts and bars.

He was scarcely gone when a peremptory knocking resounded on the street door. There was no janitor to open or to reply, so the leaves were burst asunder and two eunuchs attended by armed slaves rushed in. These surrounding the litter, removed the gag from the lady's mouth, telling her that Kynon was arrested for poisoning Prince Iorwerth, and that they had hastened to rescue her from the vengeance of the culprit's friends, rejoicing that they were not too late.

"Poisoned!—the prince poisoned! Is he dead? Tell me quickly!"

"No, lady, not dead. Happily the wretch was not able to complete his impious design. But the gracious prince is sick—very sick.

His sufferings would melt a heart of stone. All connected in any way with the business are to be tortured, Elidri among them, so your injuries will be avenged. We will not spare him."

"You will do well," the lady replied; "but now send men quickly to both ends of the lane behind this house. The man who had charge of me is in the conspiracy. Above the middle height, red hair and beard, blue eyes rather bloodshot, age thirty, a stout man wasted."

The door through which Rhys had passed was beaten from its hinges, and the house thoroughly explored. Angharad, with her own hand, stayed the detested dropping by dashing the clepsydra from its bracket, and sought for other objects on which to wreak her vengeance.

Rhys was soon dragged in, having blood on his face, and his hands tied behind him. Angharad snatched a stick from one of the eunuchs and beat her husband furiously about the head, exclaiming—

"The parts are changed. You are in my power. I cannot forgive now."

"Honoured lady," said the chief eunuch, "are we not wasting time? What is a wand in this delicate hand? Stripes from a being so celestial partake of the essence of blessing. At the palace are engines capable of wringing groans of anguish from a senseless block."

"You speak well and wisely," the lady replied. "Though I love not ugly sights, I will come and see you—on the rack."

Slaves shouldered the litter, and the short distance to the palace was quickly traversed. Entering the court of Iorwerth's quarters, Angharad commanded the slaves to stand still till her husband was passed under a low, heavy arch on the northern side of the square. Then she went to her apartment, where she caused herself to be arrayed in raiment seductively disheveled, practising the while before her hand-mirror transitions of countenance from woe and horror, to grief, astonishment, sympathy, and admiring love, without being betrayed into unseemly expansions or contractions of feature. When she was ready, an eunuch was despatched to the prince with a prayer that, if it would not imperil his precious health, she might assure herself with her own eyes that he had escaped the snare of the wicked, the infamous poisoner, who had also threatened herself; though that was indeed a matter of light consideration if weighed with the other crime he had ventured upon with such insolent audacity.

The prayer was granted, for the prince was convalescent; better indeed than he had been for several weeks, and was prepared to find amusement in the adventures at which Angharad hinted in her message, and of which he had already heard something.

Whether Iorwerth had been poisoned or not none could tell. If the sickness had been intentionally caused with a view of throwing off the malady, Kynon deserved credit and reward for his skill. But the orthodox creed at court was that the divine constitution of the prince baffled the noxious principles brought against it. Others of his dependants whispered that poisons suited his venomous temperament better than nourishing meat or wholesome medicine; but these were bad characters, who had felt the scourge of outraged justice, as their mutilated bodies and scarred limbs abundantly testified.

Angharad, on being ushered into the auspicious presence, found that a different set of variations were required, those she had practised being quite worn out. Iorwerth allowed her to support his head upon her breast while he satisfied his revived appetite, and to tell the tale of her adventures which had to be represented in a laughable instead of a pathetic aspect, to suit the caprice of the invalid.

"And how did you feel when your husband stood over you with a knife as long as my arm, and frightfully sharp? Why, he might have taken it into his mad head to pare you as you are paring that apple."

"My thoughts," replied Angharad, with a genuine, irrepressible shudder at the idea— "my reflections were much perturbed by the terrors of the situation; but below all other feelings was one mightier than the rest—a sensation of rapture that I was suffering for the sake, and at the bidding of my beloved—my adored prince."

" By all the saints," Iorwerth cried, " you shall enjoy the sensation again, and the whole court shall admire your heroic endurance! You shall be brought in bound in the same litter, there shall be a clepsydra in the corner, your husband shall sharpen the same knife, and you shall utter touching sentiments without any gag."

" True love," said Angharad, with some stiffness, " shrinks from ostentatious display, and a madman with a sharp knife is a dangerous beast, if uncontrolled. I speak not from any unworthy fears on my own account, but from a pious regard to your life, which might be endangered."

" Oh, have no fears for me, sweet one! I will observe the scene from the grated window. There shall be archers, in case he is too violent."

Perhaps a thought flashed through the woman's mind that it was an ill exchange to barter the sincere, if jealous love of a decent man, and the rough, abundant comfort of his house, for this sort of thing; but the illumination, if it came, would serve rather for punishment than for warning.

On passing through the strong gate, Rhys was turned over to the jailer, a heavy, morose brute; just the sort of man whom one would expect in such an office, which combined the safe keeping of prisoners with the duties of torturing and executing them. This man said nothing till the slaves who brought the prisoner were gone, then showing foul teeth through an opening in a foul beard, he growled—

"Ah, stout Rhys, you have been prowling about my quarters too much of late. The trap has shut on you. You have lost flesh since your wife's promotion. Never look so glum, man. Jail is not such a bad place when the jailer is your friend, as he always is to those who pay. Pay freely; think of my comforts, and I think of yours."

"That is fair," said Rhys, who knew something of the man; "but you must send my tablets to the friend who looks after my house, for I have nothing about me worth your acceptance."

"And men say you are mad. I have not heard a wiser speech for months. You write; I will see the tablets are sent. Tell them at the same time to give the bearer a jar of that famous old wine I have heard of. That will do. Now I must search you. Ha! a pretty knife to cut off ears and noses with; and a trifle of money, as you say; and a very handsome bracelet, which you wish me to keep in remembrance of this joyful meeting. Now, as to the irons. Here! slave, fool, beast—how often must I call; bring those behind the door. Massive, you think. In your ear—hollow, the lightest I have." Then, striking the slave on the head with them, "Don't you know what to do?"

The slave fetched an anvil, hammer, and rivets, and Rhys was accommodated.

"Now come along," said the jailer; "I

must put you in the common ward at first, in case any one should be sent to see you."

They went down a flight of stone steps between green, slimy walls, to a low, solid door, barred and cross-barred with rusty iron. On either side of the door was a high, grated window, and at each window appeared a haggard, dirty, unkempt human head. Over the door was another barred window which completed the arch, and from all three came a combination of sounds—growling, snarling, laughing, and a putrid fetor, worse than any cave-den of hyenas.

Bar after bar, bolt after bolt, were undone by the slave, and the thick door turned heavily on its pivots, letting out a gush of foul air that made Rhys sick. He turned round to the jailer, and whispered—

"Put me somewhere else. I cannot bear this. Name your own price."

"I tell you I can't," answered the jailer angrily. "You must bear it as you see these do. Some die of course. I will do all I can."

"But Kynon and Elidri are not here. Why can I not be with them?"

"Why can you not be with them, mad fool," snarled the jailer, "they are in the ante-room to the torture chamber. Be content."

So the prisoner under the grated window had his fetters unshackled from the ring in the wall, the place was cleaned, the ring of Rhys' fetters inserted in the shackle, and the bolt locked in.

While this was being done, Aron the jailer advanced into the gloom which a single oil lamp could but partly dispel. Rhys took advantage of his absence to extract a piece of silver from a fold of his frock which had escaped observation, and gave it to the slave, who snatched and hid it, looking at the donor with wondering eyes. He had lost the remembrance of kindness; but gratitude sprang at the unaccustomed usage,—a vague wish to retaliate the benefit.

Then Aron's harsh voice came growling from the cavernous vault—

"He is dead, sure enough. Go, slave, and send the messenger for the brethren. Lose no time about it, or your hide will suffer." Then he added, to Rhys, "If you wish to see what the torture can do, look at this fellow as he comes out. He was a Saxon spy and was racked, not at all severely (for our elegant Praefect rather despises confessions got by torture), about three weeks ago—a little more. Not a joint pulled out, only strained a little. It is a good thing he is dead, it will save the slave the trouble of feeding him. Not that he eat much. Such as he can't stand the prison fever."

The slave came back, and Aron went about some other business.

Rhys leaned against the grated window in no hopeful state of mind. He tried to think, but a drunken disorder of ideas buzzed in his brain. His most steadfast point was a capacity for wondering. He wondered how long he should be in this place; what his wife was doing; what torture was like; and how much he could bear. What Kynon had really done, and whether he would make a damaging confession; whether it was right to let his wife escape to work more wickedness and wrong. So he rambled from one thing to another, but was incapable of pinning his mind to one subject, and calculating the probabilities of death or torture.

The chances seemed rather to be in favour of his being forgotten for an indefinite period, left to linger in this pestilent dungeon. Iorwerth had renewed his health for a time at least, and had given order for his chamberlain to return to his duties, which no one else could discharge to the prince's satisfaction. The medicus, he said, might remain where he was, with the threat of torture suspended over him.

"When he has had a taste of my power," observed Iorwerth, grandly, "he will be less inclined to trifle with it. Those who have once felt the lion's claws, are seldom disposed to tempt his fangs."

As to Rhys, the prince had something better to think of than injured plebeians and their woes; his own amusements were more worthy of consideration. Angharad was afraid to ask for her husband's punishment since the proposal to rehearse the scene in Kynon's atrium. It might be—she most fervently hoped it was—a wretched joke; but it was one of the peculiarities of her beloved prince, that he liked his people to tremble as well as laugh at his lighter utterances, and if levity were too apparent some ghastly incident would often redress the balance. Evidently the less said about Rhys the better. Elidri, who was the rival of the chief eunuch in providing for their master's amusement, considered Rhys as a fellow-sufferer, and might make himself unpleasant if any open ill-treatment were practised upon him.

Rhys was recalled to practical matters by the slave who brought a bowl of water and a rag to wash the dried blood from his benefactor's face. Neither water nor bowl were very clean, but Rhys drank the turbid fluid and thanked his new friend. Speaking kindly to the lad, who seemed about eighteen, he discovered that he was a Saxon, and had been Aron's slave for a long time, apparently about ten years. He had not a friend, not even a companion. The Saxon slaves, of whom there were a few, refused to recognize him, because he had forgotten his mother tongue; while those of other races called him the Saxon fool. Perhaps he was irreclaimably stupid, perhaps more gentle nurture might have enabled him to pass muster with the average men of his class. But he had never had a chance. Before the time he became a slave, the only events which made on his mind impressions durable enough to be retained, were sundry beatings, and an occasional bellyful of acorns. As he answered in the fewest and plainest words the questions put to him, it became apparent that no most wretched dog lived a life so dull, so bare, so harassed, and so hopeless. The prisoners near at hand, squatting on their haunches, with haggard eyes staring from masses of dirt and hair, felt themselves to be superior beings. Rhys, not usually very sensitive, and having griefs of his own, yet found a place in his heart that ached at this tale of negatives. Except suffering and scorn, the past was nothing, the present nothing, and nothing was looked for from the future. Rhys, wondering perhaps what such a being would buy, asked what he intended to do with the money given him. The lad answered by producing the piece of silver from his ragged tunic, where it hung suspended from his neck by a thong. He had taken the first opportunity to make a hole with the smallest punch used for the rivets, and threaded it on to a ravel from his master's whip. The story ran all round the prison, and some laughter, and a few feeble jokes, were the result of the little incident. But mirth soon dwined away, choked by the air of the charnel-house; private regrets occupied every thought, and silent misery brooded in obscurity.

A low, monotonous strain of music was heard without, drawing gradually nearer, till it reached the top of the steps leading down to the vault. A man's voice seemed to lead, singing a verse, the boys and others chiming in as memory served; then a second voice chanted the next verse, accompanied in like manner. The first words clearly heard were—

"Eduxit eos de tenebris et umbra mortis; et vincula eorum disrupit."

"Confiteantur Domino misericordiae ejus," but a surly voice broke in——

"You have leave to visit the prison, and to plague the sick and dying, also to remove the dead, but there is nothing said about extraneous howling."

"We are only thanking God," Eleutherius said, with some asperity, "that by death he has released a wretched Christian from your hands."

"My hands," cried Aron, wrathfully, "wretched Christian—a spy, a double—both sides traitor! Just the villain you priests sympathize with."

"He was better than you," Eleutherius retorted, "in that he repented——"

But John interposed, holding out the cross he carried, saying—

"We know our privilege, and will not overstep it by brawling. We bring to the wretched, the sick, the dying, glad tidings of peace."

"Hominibus bonae voluntatis," growled Eleutherius in a lower tone.

"Of peace, brother," John continued; "and there is in this message a special blessing on the peacemakers. Let the boy with the thurible go forward, for the air of this place is terrible to old lungs."

The boy went down the slippery steps swinging a latten incense pot, and was followed by another bearing a vessel of holy water.

As the procession entered the dungeon some of the inmates knelt, some stood in attitudes more or less respectful, some remained crouching on the damp stones, muttering curses. The priests gave their blessing to all, and went to the place where the dead man lay on a little rotten straw.

The body was placed on a light bier, and Rhys noticed, as it passed him, that the wrists and ankles were covered with wounds, where the cords of the rack had torn the skin.

At the door John turned and addressed the prisoners—

"My children—God has struck off the chains of a captive, and delivered him from all the pains and troubles of the world. Great were the sins of him whose body we have carried out from your midst, but greater is the mercy of Him who pardons the penitent. Do you, who are left here, 'sitting in darkness and the shadow of death,' seek that mercy in humility, penitence, and faith? My heart bleeds to witness your sufferings in this loathsome den. But oh, the prison-house of Satan is a thousand times more intolerable than this: the wretchedness of sin is worse than all that man can inflict. Praises and thanksgivings have ascended from the dungeon; the foulest places of the earth may be sweetened by the incense of prayer. There is a freedom none can take from you ; a joy no outward circumstances can control."

So the old man talked to them, and prayed earnestly, but on most hearts there was a crust of dull despair his words could not soften.

The procession went away singing "Miserere mei Deus ;" and Gorr the forester was buried with such rites as beseemed. He was professedly penitent, and the priests allowed him as such, though they could not feel very confident about him. They played the strict game, and scorned to cheat even the old adversary, but they would not yield a doubtful point. Owing to the restrictions placed on their visits to the jail, John and Eleutherius had not been able to do all they wished, and they endeavoured to make up for the omissions by prayers for the welfare of the departed.

CHAPTER IX.

THE diversion made by the foresters and the men of Gwent on the night of the storming of the bridge-head had been easily repulsed by Cissa. Farinmail's sickness had dispirited his own men and deprived the more irregular bands of their only acknowledged head. Orders were obeyed or not, as suited the convenience or caprice of each subordinate leader. That very day messengers had arrived from Caradoc desiring the immediate return of his son to Venta, and the troops flatly refused to remain before Anderida without him. The foresters who had consumed their resources of food and missiles, began to melt away like a mist of the morning, when they heard of the intended departure of their allies.

There was one point to be settled before Farinmail could leave those parts with propriety. He now lay on a rustic couch of fir-tassels in a pleasant arbour, discussing the matter with Comail.

"You see," said the sick man, "the challenge was fairly given between the hosts, and I cannot without reproach leave it unanswered."

"Of course," Comail replied, "you cannot do anything in your present state. However, there is no difficulty about it. I can take your place as you have taken mine many a time."

"I do not know whether the Saxon customs in such affairs are the same as ours. Æscwine may say that fighting with you will not settle his quarrel with me. That is perhaps the view which would recommend itself to the uninstructed, natural man."

"Morbid fancies!" exclaimed Comail. "Æscwine will not say anything of the sort. The natural man, if he is a good fellow, fights the best man he can get, without making needless difficulties. In fact the more noble among the brutes do the same; if there is no old quarrel to conclude when they meet, they make a new one. However, to avoid all possibility of error or misunderstanding, it shall be distinctly proclaimed that this is merely a whet, and that as soon as you can bear your armour, the very feast shall come off."

"I do not want any buffoonery brought into the affair," Farinmail said pettishly. Then, after a minute's silence, holding out his hand, "Forgive me, cousin. If I recover from these hurts it will be due mainly to your care, and your never-failing good temper and spirits."

"If you recover. No more such ifs as that, if you please. It is these cursed swamps that hinder your cure. I wish you could have that medicus of Iorwerth's who was so badly treated after the battle. I will mention the man's name when I write to Æscwine; probably Ælle will agree to a few hours' truce, and the ladies can come to the meeting place. Perhaps a few more young fellows on both sides would like to try their dexterity and the edge of their swords. By the temple of Concord, I shall have to fight on foot!"

"Not while I have a horse. But what ails your own?"

"It is not that. These Saxons fight always on foot. Well, there is the old saying, 'A mare's son may fail me; my father's son will never fail me.' When one cannot do as well as one would, one must do as well as one can. Now for the epistle, in your best style."

"I should begin something in this way. 'Farinmail of Venta to Æscwine the Gesith, friendship and greeting. Being at present sick and unable to bear my armour, I have not as yet been able to reply worthily to the invitation you gave between the hosts——'"

"Would you not use some title of respect at the outset?" Comail interrupted; 'Æscwine the Gesith' sounds rather—rather bare."

"It is his proper appellation, and must be

employed in a formal missive. You notice that I use no title of honour myself, lest it should seem ungracious—'hosts on the night' —What night was it?"

"It was the morning the long bridge was burned, or before; one could hardly tell whether it was night or morning. Say the day before the Calends of July. Do they not call June the Hay month? They count by moons. I remember the young moon was first seen on the Ides of June, and it was new the fourth day before the Ides, but how they count——"

"Better say the day before the Calends of July," said Farinmail, "we shall know what we mean, and that is no small advantage in written communications, even if all others fail to understand us."

So the letter was written between them, and a runner took it to Æscwine.

Now Ælle, as soon as he felt himself secure, had sent for his daughters from Wlencing, and with them came other ladies and their attendants, and log-houses were built for them in the fort formerly occupied by the men of Gwent, and suitable guard appointed. When therefore Æscwine got his letter and did not know what to do about it, he, like a wise man, took it to Ostrythe. Ostrythe sat in a bower of branches on the southern wall of the fort looking toward the sea; Eanfled, with two others, was there chatting pleasantly, as the salt wind rustled the leaves. They were glad of the change from Wlencing, and perhaps hoped for some adventures to relieve the monotony of spinning and weaving, and for a change, making others weave and spin.

"What is amiss with Æscwine?" Eanfled asked, as the young man came along the rampart biting his moustache, bending angry looks on a square, flat, white thing which he held in his hand.

"It is only something the Lord Farinmail has sent me," said Æscwine.

"Oh, what is it?" Ostrythe exclaimed. "Is it a Welsh falcon? I love the Welsh falcons, they are so proud, and beautiful, and gentle."

"I have brought it to you that you may tell me what it is;" saying which, Æscwine tossed the epistle into Ostrythe's lap. She opened it.

"Is this all?" she asked in tones of disappointment. "What do these marks mean? Runes I suppose. No bad magic, I hope."

"Lord Farinmail would not stoop to anything of that sort. He has something to say to me, and I would find out what it is."

"Ask the man who brought it," suggested Eanfled, "perhaps he knows."

"I asked him. He told me that it was a missive from the Lord Farinmail, but that he was entirely ignorant of its contents."

"It is very foolish," Ostrythe remarked, "to send such things without some one to explain their meaning. I should have thought the Lord Farinmail would have known better. But I hear he is sick."

"There goes a man who can tell us all about it," one of the ladies said.

Looking down into the fort they saw a long, lean man striding away with his body stretched forward, as if it were the great object of his desire that his nose should reach some given point before the rest of his person. Æscwine shouted, "Cnebba! Cnebba! come up hither. A matter of great importance."

When the sorcerer saw the party above, he came up the path.

"Can you read these runes for us?" Æscwine inquired solemnly.

"I can," replied the conjuror in his most serious voice, whereat the ladies moved in their seats with feelings of satisfaction.

"This rune which you see here is the first on the list, it represents the sound aa. If you wish to show the sound aa in visible shape you make this rune. This sign in like manner is the symbol of the sound ee. When you wish to make ee——"

"All this," Ostrythe said, interrupting him, "may be very useful to sheep or mice, but we do not want to say aa, or ee, in any shape; we wish to know the message sent in this absurd fashion. If he had told it to the runner, he might have had his answer by this. Now, never mind your aa and ee. The message."

"Lady," said the man of learning, "they who desire knowledge must begin at the beginning. The art of making words visible——"

"How long will it take to get through all this about aa and ee?"

"It took me about seven years," Cnebba replied, "but I could——"

"The shortest way then," Æscwine said, "will be to send back the messenger, and beg the Lord Farinmail to let us have an interpreter. The man can go and return in two hours at most."

Cnebba resented the want of deference shown him, and threw no more light on the document, which he could have read after a fashion, and would have done so, had he not been withheld by the feeling, that any mistake he might fall into would assuredly be found out.

When the runner returned to the British

camp and told his message, Farinmail and his cousin looked at each other for some moments, and broke into a simultaneous laugh. When it was over—

"We need not have been so exact about the Calends of July," said the former. "What shall we do? It will need weeks to settle the business if messengers must go to and fro about every detail."

"I will go myself," said Comail, "as interpreter. It is the only way."

"That you shall not," replied his cousin. "You would take very good care of my interests; but I cannot trust you to look after your own."

"Suppose we both go. Everything can be settled so, without loss of time or possibility of mistake; and we can fight to-morrow morning."

So the pair set off. Farinmail in a litter with four bearers, and Comail riding by his side. They were passed in at the gate of the fort as the interpreter and his assistant, and after a little delay were taken to the bower of branches looking toward the sea.

If the Saxons were astonished on discovering who the interpreters were, the Britons, on their side, felt a little embarrassment at the having to introduce the subject of their mission to such a company. They tried to make it a confidential communication, but in vain; the curiosity of the ladies was aroused, and was not to be baulked.

Farinmail put a good face on it; and with two or three neatly turned compliments to Æscwine, told how he was obliged to return to Venta, and that his cousin would be proud to carry out the engagement which he could not fulfil, in consequence of his broken health.

The truth of the latter part of the speech was evidenced by the pale, hollow cheek and wasted hand. Ostrythe drew her seat beside the litter, and Eanfled sent her maiden for wine. The latter returned, before she had gone five paces, to inform her mistress that Ælle the King was at that moment coming up the sloping path which led to the top of the rampart. The thought of what her father-in-law might say or do, when he found so formidable an enemy in his grasp, frightened Eanfled. There was only one way of managing him, and she ran to meet the king, in hopes of coaxing a promise from him after telling the truth."

She met the king behind the bower, and said, without disguising her fears: "Unexpected guests have just come to us, father. I do not know what welcome you will give them. It is our fault that they came."

"There is a fault, then," Ælle said, in a deep, rough voice. "Do not fear that I shall be harsh with you, Enede—that is not my wont."

"Nor is it my wont to fear, you, at least on my own account."

"For whom do you fear, then? What is the fault? In few words."

"In few words, then, father: Farinmail of Venta is here, half dead in a litter. I have sent for some wine for him. The other is Comail; he whom Ostrythe wounded in the shoulder with her spear."

"They of all men," Ælle growled through his beard. "Why are they come?"

"They are come to invite Æscwine to a duel to-morrow at sunrise. Æscwine challenged Farinmail a few weeks ago, and as Farinmail is too weak to bear armour, they propose that Comail shall take his cousin's place. They are summoned home, and do not like to return to Venta without fulfilling the engagement. They sent a letter which we could not read, and desired an interpreter of them; whereupon they came themselves. So you see it is our fault."

"They need not trouble their minds about the return to Venta."

With these words, Ælle came from behind the bower of branches, Eanfled holding his big, hard, hairy hand in both her own.

For a minute or so no one spoke, but all eyes were fixed on the unsophisticated savage from beyond the northern sea; a heathen, an eater of horse-flesh—perhaps worse— Ostrythe smiled and spoke—

"We are entertaining two bodes, who have come in somewhat irregular fashion."

"These come not as bodes should come. I hold them not as such."

Farinmail tried to raise himself, but Ostrythe laid her hand upon him; and when he turned to her with mute appeal, said in a low voice—

"Not yet. I will not hinder you when fit time comes."

"Young men," said Ælle sternly, "you are come here to-day, as you came into my land a moon and a half agone, without any of the outward signs cu tomary among yourselves on such occasions. As to the value of such signs, I say nothing, but every show of respect you use to each other shall be paid to me; if not, look to yourselves."

"We do not use toward the wild boar——" but a hand was laid on Farinmail's mouth. The Saxon King had no difficulty in finishing the speech.

"If you scorn the boar, beware of his tusk. Your own folk would not recognize you as bodes coming in this wise, nor shall I. You are fools to put yourselves in my power after what you have done. I shall not be such a fool as to let you go. Your punishment shall be a warning to others not to deal so with me. Without provocation, without warning, you come upon the lands of my people; you slay them, you burn their houses, lay waste their fields, destroy their crops, take their chattels. For this injury to them, for this insult to myself, vengeance is due. If before I speak your doom you have anything to say for yourselves I will hear you."

And Ælle the King looked far away, with eyes as immovable as the hills on which they rested. Nevertheless, when Ostrythe put her strong white arm under Farinmail's head, and raised him up, with words of encouragement, her father said in a tone of surprise—

"My child, do you uphold and comfort one who is my enemy?"

"Dear father," Ostrythe replied, lifting her bright face toward him; "I was this sick man's prisoner. My ransom has not been paid. I must work it out or I shall be shamed."

A shade of vexation passed over the face of the Saxon King. Ostrythe was the only person in the world who could come between him and his prey, and she evidently was determined to do it.

He set his face more doggedly than before, and Farinmail began—

" Fourteen years ago, Lord King, without warning, without provocation, you came to these shores to burn, to slay, to pillage, on the lands of my people. That we should stand by our own, is that a crime? Would it not rather be the vilest guilt to turn a deaf ear to the cry of our brethren? But why should I plead—to what purpose do you hear? Is it from any desire to do justice? No, the wolf's plea is good enough for you."

" I am just," Ælle replied, "though perhaps our notions of right differ. You have wronged me, and have put yourselves in my power."

" In your power—yes. But what is your

power? Is it founded on right? No; it is and it rests on nothing but wrong and robbery. Every mile of your territory, the very turf on which you stand to talk of right and justice, has been snatched by violence from the rightful owner. Your justice, it is wolf's law; your right is only might."

"I know no other, right," answered Ælle, calmly, "and you follow no other rule. By strength of limb, and strength of heart, and strength of brain, you have made the horse and the hawk your servants, and they help you to slay the feeble tribes for your food and clothing. Have you no slaves? By what right do you hold them but that of the strongest? Surely the law which is good for them is good for you."

"There is a right of conquest, doubtless, but it is not the only one; there is the right of justice, which our fellow-men claim of us as they claim our mercy; the feeble have a right to our protection."

"As to the feeble," laughed Ælle, "if they come meekly to my feet, I spare them, unless there is some reason to do otherwise. The other rights you speak of are rights if one can enforce them. What good are rights which cannot be enforced? they are dead—nothing. A brave man loves truth, justice, open fighting; because lying, cheating, secret murder, are the weapons of cowards; moreover, truth, justice, good faith, make the strong man stronger; but strength is the only right at last."

"But is the strong to take everything? All will be stronger than any one."

"There is strength in wisdom. The strongest must be wise."

"There is, most likely, a stronger than you. What will you do if he come?"

"If a stronger comes and bends me, I shall be bent. He has not come yet."

"Your gods are stronger than yourself, they can bend you."

"I know not that," Ælle said, without any appearance of boasting. "Strong men have contended with the gods and prevailed. Perhaps they love the man who does not fear them, and will not put out their strength against him."

"Is there, then, nothing you admit to be stronger than yourself?"

"The Thunderer wrestled with Old-age in Utgard, and she brought him to his knee. She will bend me, and death will lay me low. The gods cannot deliver me from death. I sacrifice to them as the fathers did of old, but I trust in my own strength, skill, and hardihood."

"I fancy," said Farinmail, "that pagan Romans held the same creed."

"Romans," the king repeated, "Romans, that is the name in the song of Hereman. They used to sing it in the winter, when the logs blazed in the middle of the hall; where snowflakes floated down, melting as they fell; where sparrows flew in from the hungry frost and fought for crumbs on the floor. Those were winters indeed. Hereman slew the Romans in swamps of the forest sacred to Tiw. The gloomy shades were gleaming with heaps of bones; horse-skulls grinned from the lopped trees. Meaner captives hung on gibbets, the leaders were slain on the altar of Tiw, as—" the king continued, without any change of voice, "as I think to slay you. A sacrifice would be pleasing to the one-handed War-god, and he might help us to take the city. At any rate it could do no harm."

The two Britons, bold even to recklessness, were rather startled at this way of putting it. There was a repugnance to the idea of being sacrificed to a miserable idol; a shrinking from a fate so bestial, which the mere idea of death was powerless to produce.

"May I ask, Lord King, if you think to eat us afterwards?" Comail said.

"It is the custom," Ælle replied, "to eat part of the sacrifice. I dislike the practice, as making no difference between men and beasts; but the old warriors like it, and the priests say it is due to the god. It is not worth while to thwart them in so small a matter."

Comail would have sprung at the king's

throat and tried his boasted strength, if Farinmail had been in a condition to second him. But success would have been no success, unless the cousins got away together, and as the project arose, the need for it passed away. Ostrythe gently laid Farinmail down, then, with burning cheeks, she rose and spoke out—

"Father, how can you think such things? Wolves do not eat wolves."

"Not in summer," Ælle replied; "but when the northern winds bring snow, and snow brings hunger, and hunger brings——"

"But you and your old warriors and old priests do not eat for hunger."

"Well, well. The eating can be given up if you think so much of it."

"And the sacrifice can be given up. Help you to take the great fortress—you who trust in your own skill and strength! You are not in earnest, you cannot be: the words will not fit together. But I am in earnest. If anything happen to these two, I shall kill myself for very shame. I was in their power, and they treated me nobly; so shall they be treated. Your old wolves must at least be as civil as the brutes."

"Dare you speak disrespectfully to me. Does my love deserve———"

"I do not speak undutifully. Your true self, the self which loves me, I love and obey gladly;—but, dear father, you are hard, but not unjust. You owe these princes life for our lives; honourable treatment in return for their kindness. What will men say?"

"I care little for their sayings."

"You care much for power, and the good word of the worthy is strength. Besides, did you not promise me a gift at midsummertide, what I chose to ask."

"You had the golden chestnut."

"Yes, and he goes like a bird; but you know—you know I did not ask for him. I ask for these two, and you cannot refuse."

Ostrythe was coaxing on one side, Eanfled on the other; and Ælle, yielding partly to their persuasions, partly to his sense of right, grumbled—

"Take them, then; and now that is settled. Let me go."

"Pardon me, Lord King," said Æscwine. "Before you go, will you declare your will about the fight, the holm-gang."

"Waste of time," exclaimed Ælle. "Waste of life. We fight for serious matters, for lands to feed us, and houses to dwell in. We do not fly at each other's throats without cause, as dogs do, or wolves—eh! daughter. Shall your betrothed fight like a wolf? Shall he be no better than the brutes?"

"He must decide such matters for himself," Ostrythe replied coolly. "If he cannot take care of himself he will not do for me. Men must not be wolves, but they must be men."

So the duel was fixed for the next morning at sunrise; and the place chosen was the natural theatre where the first scene of the triumph took place.

While the preliminaries were being arranged, Ostrythe begged her father to send for Kynon from the city to prescribe for Farinmail.

"Not," she said, "that anything better can be done than to give him plenty of water, in which bark of white willows has been boiled, and to send him up among the hills."

"Have you done?" Ælle asked, "or is there anything else you want?"

"I should like exceedingly," Ostrythe answered, "to hear the song of Hereman."

CHAPTER X.

A SHORT time after noon of the same day a messenger from Ælle, and a request from Farinmail, were brought to Julius, demanding the presence of the leech Kynon. Farinmail's tablets told in few words the reasons for his recall from the field, and added a hope that he should soon be able to return with renewed strength and increased forces. The withdrawal of the men of Gwent was not unforeseen; but prescience cannot make an unwelcome draught less bitter in the mouth, and Julius felt but slight interest in the cause whose proper champions left him to bear the stress of battle alone. He hardened his heart, trusting only to himself, and to the solid Roman wall.

Four of the Praefect's guard went to the

prison to release the medicus, and the jailer with his slave attended them to the cell to unbar the doors, to unlock the shackle, and to unrivet the fetters and manacles. Then, with unshorn beard and matted hair tangled with straw, his clothes smeared with slime of obscene things which are begotten of damp and darkness, his thoughts broody with wrath and revenge, Kynon was marched through the streets to the house of the Praefect. Arrived there, he was questioned as to the cause of his imprisonment, but the thin bristly lips refused to open.

The officer of the guard explained that there was a conspiracy against the life of Prince Iorwerth, whom Kynon had attempted to poison.

"An attempt," said the Praefect. "Why did it not succeed? However, you are wanted now to attend the Lord Farinmail, so go home and put yourself to rights. How soon can you be ready? The Saxon King sends you a safe conduct, but I do not quite understand it all."

Kynon opened his mouth, and spoke in short, jerky sentences—

"I make no attempts. If I had wished to poison him, would he be now alive? I relieved him from the consequences of his vicious conduct. As a recompense I was immured in a pestiferous hole; threatened with torture; my house wrecked. Do you hope to have the benefit of my art, my skill, my experience, on terms such as these? You will not."

"Do as you please," Julius replied. "It is no interest of mine. Indeed, I dislike going and coming between hostile camps, as a rule."

A shapeless idea of vengeance began to curdle in a dark corner of Kynon's mind at these words. To gain time for its development, he said—

"It is irritating to the feelings of a scholar and a man of art to be sent hither and thither like a bale of merchandise. But I do not refuse the succour of science to those in need of it. Moreover, there is a difference in the nature of the two patients. I shall require an hour or two to set my house in order. Also, I must have an opportunity of private conference with the man Rhys, who has had charge of certain moneys and commodities of mine. He is in the northern vaults on the same charge as myself."

"You shall see him," Julius said; "and I will look into the whole matter with my own eyes. Justice shall be done to him and to you also. There is a warning I must give you. If you talk of our state as to military or other matters in the Saxon camp I shall most likely hear of it. Faults of that kind are severely punished. Better say nothing."

"Mouth shut, ears and eyes open, Lord Praefect—that is the rule for a medicus."

Kynon, attended by a servant of the magistrate, went towards the northern vaults, brooding as he went over his unshapen idea. One part or another seemed to be acquiring solidity; but there was as yet no form or definite outline. They came to the jailer's lodging, and the authority for seeing Rhys in private being displayed, the slave was sent with the medicus, while the attendant remained behind to question Aron. That worthy at first refused information, saying that it was a palace matter, and that the Praefect had no authority within those bounds. The apparitor calmly replied to this assertion—

"You will be very much your own enemy if you send such a message as that to the Lord Praefect. You know that he never admitted the validity of such a pretension in Vortipore's most palmy time; and now the authority of the Count is really vested in Julius Romanus, whose power you will not venture to question."

The jailer had not the slightest intention of so doing, and had merely protested for the sake of gaining a little time.

"Ay, ay," he said, "one forgets sometimes what a hoist you fellows got at the last turn of the wheel. What do you want to know?"

"I require information as to the authority

by which you were justified in committing Rhys to jail. I must *see* the authority."

Aron felt intense satisfaction as he gave to the apparitor not the warrant on which Rhys was actually committed which was signed by the chief eunuch, but one previously put in his hands by Elidri in case the culprit who haunted the terrace and who dropped a knife into the Prince's couch, should be discovered; in which warrant Rhys was named as the suspected person.

"But this," said the apparitor, "is dated three weeks ago. Why the delay?"

"They did not like to act without more than suspicion to go upon."

"This is not countersigned on committal."

"Elidri was arrested an hour before Rhys was brought in. The latter was caught by chance in the house of Kynon when the men went to rescue the Lady Angharad. It is only because the two prisoners were committed at the same time, that the ignorant suppose it was for the same offence. You see the thing speaks for itself. Elidri would not have ordered Rhys to jail for conspiring with himself. Rhys could have betrayed the plot—of course he could."

"Then I am to understand that Rhys was committed by order of Elidri, for trespassing by night in the palace, contrary to the law; but Elidri was imprisoned with Kynon by a different authority, on suspicion of a conspiracy to poison the prince?"

"That is it; but you express it much more clearly than I can do."

The apparitor smiled graciously at this tribute to his trained skill, and the jailer grinned to think how a little ready homespun had kept in his hands a very profitable customer. To clench the business, he gave the official a horn of Rhys' wine.

Kynon's motive in making a point of obtaining a private interview with Rhys was not clear even to himself. He knew that they both detested Iorwerth, and hoped, perhaps, that the collision of hatreds might lead to something, for malice is almost as fertile in expedients as love. He found

Rhys in a depressed condition. He was, by comparison, clean and comfortable, and was supplied with abundance of good food and wine which he shared freely with those nearest to him. He chafed at the restraint, and felt a sort of wild beast craving to wander and hunt his prey.

Kynon tried to cheer him, saying that Julius would do him justice. "I shall find you at liberty when I come back, and then——"

"Back! Where are you going? Everyone seems to fall away from me."

"I shall not be long away. I am only sent for to cure the Lord Farinmail, who is sick. Ælle gives me safe conduct through his camp."

"Will you see Smith by the way, and tell him that I am locked up?"

"I cannot promise to do that," said Kynon; "in fact the Praefect warned me of the risk of attempting anything of the sort."

"I can tell you how to do it without risk," Rhys whispered. "Hang round your neck a token I will furnish you with. It can be hidden inside your coat till you see him. You know him by sight."

"Yes, I know him, but I may not see him. What is this token?"

"It is a pair of keys. I will give you an order for them on my tablets. You are sure to meet him. Show the keys, and leave the rest to him."

"That I will do. But what are these wonder-working keys?"

"That," said Rhys, "is a secret, but I must tell it to you."

As Rhys revealed the mystery, the chaotic atoms of hate floating in darkness became cosmic, grouped themselves in families, and lived and grew in orderly, harmonious sequence and connection.

Two hours afterwards Kynon was in the Saxon camp, waiting for guides and escort to the camp of Farinmail. A small crowd stood near the principal booth, listening to an Anglian glee-man, who sang, to a dismal tune—

"Where in wide ocean *
Wanders the whale-brood
Dwelleth in deep woods
Of a dim island
The mystic mother—
Nerthe the mighty,
Covered with curtains
In her car resting.
Death is the doom of him
Daring to touch aught
Sacred to Nerthe,
Save the priest only.
Through the wood whispering
Windeth a warning—
In her car cow-drawn
Nerthe is coming,
Festive, but fearful
Must the priest follow.
Lucky the days,
Lucky the lands are,
When Nerthe cometh,
Where Nerthe bideth.
War is forsworn,
Swords are forgotten,
Peace wields the people
With rest and pleasure,
Till the mild mother,
Mortals forsaking,

---

* Tac. Ger. 40.

> Home to the deep woods
> In her car wendeth.
> There in a lost lake
> Lurking mid thick trees,
> Wash they the car,
> The curtains, the Goddess.
> But the task ended,
> The washers are taken
> Swiftly from life
> By the lake swallowed.
> Silent and sacred
> The sleep of the Goddess."

Kynon paid no heed to the song; his eyes were roving here and there, searching for Smith. It was not till he shifted his position so as to look round a projecting corner of the great booth that the object of his quest was discovered talking to a small man, who was a stranger to the medicus. The unknown was Ent, who noticed Kynon's steady gaze, and called his friend's attention to the Briton.

Smith was just come from his forge; his face and bare hairy arms were begrimed with smoke, and his high leathern apron singed by the hot scales of iron. Kynon displayed the keys for a moment, pressed his lips together with his finger and thumb, then turned away to the other side of the crowd. Presently a low voice said—

"You have something to say to me in private."

"Yes, our meeting must be not only out of hearing, but out of sight."

"I understand; it shall be so as far as is needful. You may trust that little man whom you saw with me; he knows all about the keys. Give yourself no concern; I will arrange matters."

Shortly after this, Kynon was summoned into the principal booth, on one of the long sides whereof Ælle sat superintending the distribution of rings. His seat was a massive oaken bench rudely carved with foliage and grotesque monsters. On the back of the settle, an artist of unusual skill had exercised his powers.* A warrior seated on a rock held on his knees the head of another who seemed to be wounded; on one side

* See Beowulf.

writhed a dragon with a sword sticking in its body, another blade lying broken on the ground, while curls of smoke issued from the mouth and the wounds of the firedrake; on the other side was a heap of dishes, drinking-vessels, and ornaments, in front of the entrance to a cavern. One arm of the wide throne exhibited a grim being tearing off the shoulder of a creature even more grisly; the other showed a terrific sword-stroke descending on the neck of a female monster. The king sat on this noble seat, with the chiefs and elders on the right hand and on the left. On the opposite side of the hall was another raised bench, without any carving, destined for guests whom the king wished especially to honour, and in the midst, between the two, was the hearth, now cold. In front of the king sat four Gesithas paying the allies. This was the distribution of rings. In early times it was the custom of chiefs to reward their followers with gifts of rings, bracelets, torques, and other ornaments, and so they still did on special occasions. But the Saxons had learned the use of coined money, and found it convenient. The word ring was loosely used, and these round pieces of metal marked with the outline of a wolf's head in honour of Tiw, were as near an approach to the shape as were the cervical vertebrae of a giantess, which were poetically called her bone rings. The men frequently cast their money into rings and armlets, as the safest method of carrying it when on an expedition.

The tything-men of Osmund the Jute were receiving their arrears of pay when Kynon entered. He was passed on till he came to the platform on which the king sat. Smith, no longer grimy, stood in his place among the chiefs, and was speaking earnestly to Ælle. Kynon paid his respects in due form.

"You are the leech," said the king, "going to Farinmail of Venta."

"I am, Lord King. If I can be of service to any of your people, I will do what in me lies, for science is of no country."

"Ah," said Ælle, "indeed. I hate your no-country folk. Every man should stick to his kin and his neighbours who are pledges for him. He who has no surety for himself is most likely a rogue."

The Saxons standing by applauded the sentiment, and the medicus not understanding the system of pledges and sureties which made a society responsible for the conduct of each of its members, saw at least that his offer was not well received, and said no more.

"I suppose," Ælle went on, "you were bidden to take back a report of all you can see or hear. You are welcome to pick up what you can, but no tampering with my people."

The medicus was not sorry to get out of the king's presence.

Then Smith led him to the place where five of Farinmail's horsemen awaited him. They mounted and rode through forest ways, followed by Smith and two Gesithas. The afternoon was still young when the healer was introduced to Farinmail, who lay on pine-tassels drinking with heroism floods of water in which bark of the white willow had been boiled.

"It is not a bad remedy, though an old woman's," said Kynon.

"An old woman!" cried Farinmail, "the lady Ostrythe an old woman! Crimen laesae majestatis; treason and blasphemy."

"No, no," answered Kynon, "I meant that the remedy was discovered by an old woman. I often employ it myself."

Having appeased the wrath of his patient, the medicus proceeded to examine him carefully. Then, after a pause, he said—

"If there be in Venta a pharmacopola who can make the malagma of Apollophanes, let it be applied; if not, a plaster of pitch, ammoniacum, and suet will do nearly as well. Till you arrive at home, your body shall be swathed in a cloth moistened with equal parts of turpentine and oil, and daily the oil shall be more and the turpentine less; the cloth to be a foot in width. To purge the body of stagnant blood you shall swallow, night and morning, one spoonful of a certain theriaca of my own composition, a marvellous —an admirable medicine. Not one of the ingredients is to be found within a thousand leagues of this place, except the toad, and that is not——"

"Do you think," said Farinmail, "that I will swallow toads."

"Not toads, my good Lord," said the medicus eagerly, "not even a whole toad, at least not all at once, and the toad so purified, and sublimated, and refined by art. Pray do not refuse, my very excellent Lord. The method is sure; for as one fire puts out another, so one poison—— Hear me, I beseech you——"

But Farinmail was deaf to the voice of the charmer, and told the healer that he was under a vow never to admit within his lips any part of an eel, a duck, or a toad, and this vow he meant to keep. So Kynon, having been rewarded with a golden ring and other gifts, was dismissed, but the refusal of his patient to take the theriaca rankled in his heart. He rode in silence till they came to the open land.

"Well, now," said Smith, "what is it? Here we may speak freely; there is no cover for listeners, and the companions are out of hearing."

"I will put the matter before you. A man of your intelligence, though unacquainted with the art, will have no difficulty in understanding it. The septum transversum has been bruised, and corrupted blood is poisoning the springs of life. Now, as we know that one fire puts out another, so I have ascertained that one poison——"

"In the name of the wolf," Smith exclaimed, "what is this jargon? What have I to do with corrupted blood, and fire, and poison? I supposed, seeing the token, that you had a message from Rhys."

"So I have," answered Kynon, "but I thought you would like to hear about this foolish prejudice of the Lord Farinmail. It would have been most interesting, for he has a good constitution, and those on whom I have tried the specific hitherto were poor creatures who died of their complaints before the divine composition had time to display its life-giving power."

"I will take some of it myself if you like, but we can speak of that afterwards. What has friend Rhys to say to me."

"He desired me to tell you that he cannot meet you the day after to-morrow as agreed, because he is locked up in jail."

"Ah!" Smith exclaimed, "I need not ask why he is in bondage."

"You see," Kynon went on, "that he considers me his friend, by his trusting me with these keys. I am a warm friend and a warm enemy. There is nothing too good for those I love; and nothing too bad—nothing I would not do to be revenged on those I hate."

Smith noticed the vindictive look which gave point to the words, and felt that they referred to special injury. He also remembered that "science is of no country;" and he replied—

"That is just like me. There's nothing I would not do to punish the man who has wronged me. Rhys is a good fellow, and would take deep vengeance. But he is not strong enough to do right upon his foe. I offered him the means of vengeance, but he shrank, at least he delayed using them."

"Rhys is fanciful, and so misses his aim. For a tithe of the provocation he has had, I would have wrapped a city in flames, and quenched the fire with the blood of those who had wronged me."

"That is spoken like a man. If Rhys had had that spirit his foot would have been on the head of his enemy, enemies I may say, instead of himself lying at their mercy in a prison."

"And how did you propose to help him?" the medicus asked.

"Oh, just a score or two of my friends, on whom I could rely, were to be brought in by means of those keys. We make our way to the quarters of the prince, secure him and the woman, fire the palace, and make good our retreat in the confusion."

"Yes," Kynon said with much deliberation, "he would be well avenged in that way. He thought, I suppose, that the business might be carried farther than he wished; might be too thorough."

"I cannot guess his motive," Smith replied. "I would not make such an offer to every one, for I and my friends would run a fearful risk. Rhys I could trust, but still it would have been a terrible risk."

"It would, indeed. It was a noble proof of friendship. In Rhys' place I should have accepted the offer with thankfulness."

"You are a man of high spirit," Smith said carelessly. "No one would injure you as Rhys was injured, and escape unhurt."

"I also have been wronged," Kynon said with a savage emphasis. "I would give ample pledges to any who—time is short—I know what you mean. I shall not flinch. These people are nothing to me. I came here a stranger but a few years since, and have received for my services the dog's portion—a kick and a bone. Will Ælle consent? He seemed to be bitterly prejudiced against me—I know not why."

"That was my doing, to throw spies off the scent. I knew from your signal that your message was secret, and guessed that you would be watched. And now we had better talk no more together, for we are drawing near to the camp. I will meet you to-morrow night, if that will suit you, at the little door."

"I cannot be there to-morrow, but the next night, an hour after midnight—how will the moon be? About the first quarter?"

"About that I believe. An hour after midnight I will be there."

"Have your friends within call, no one can tell when the chance may occur, and if we let it slip, it comes never again."

"That is true," Smith observed carelessly. "Well, I will have a few at hand. But nothing has been said yet about——"

"About compensation for any losses I may

sustain, you would say. We do not know yet what they may amount to. I suppose if my house and property are destroyed, some one will make it good."

"Undoubtedly. Now, farewell; an hour after midnight."

So Kynon departed from the Saxons, and Smith went to Ælle and told him all that had taken place. The king was lost in thought.

"Is the man to be trusted?" he said, after an interval of silence.

"Lord King," Smith answered, "such men are seldom trustworthy."

"No," Ælle replied quickly, "the question is usually, are they serving themselves in serving us. So far we may safely trust them."

"He seems to be set on revenge. What he said about compensation was said as if he wished to put out of sight something he did not like to look upon. I know he was badly used by Iorwerth."

"We must risk something, of course.

There will be difficulty in bringing in a large body of men without discovery. Fifty or sixty sent round to open the great gates would be as good as a thousand. I shall think about it. An assault in the daytime, to weary them and weaken them, would be useful. Meantime, not a word to any one about these matters. I know I can trust you."

"Hap helps the hardy," said Smith with a laugh.

CHAPTER XI.

AGAIN a blythe company was gathered in the meadow which was the first stage of Vortipore's ill-advised triumph. The sun rose half an hour later than on that occasion, but the heat was more intense, and dew and gossamer united to promise a scorching day. Farinmail was borne hither and thither in his litter, superintending at all points, taking good heed that his cousin should receive no detriment through his neglect. On the curving sides of the hill which overlooked the field, as the seats of a theatre overlook the stage, were British and Saxon spectators, divided from each other by a line of stakes beyond which neither side was to go.

On the flat was Ælle on horseback, with

Ostrythe, Eanfled, and the rest of the ladies, together with almost the whole body of the Gesithas. Farinmail's horsemen, in full armour, completed the circle.

In the centre was a ring staked out, where the champions stood—the Briton on the northern side, and the Saxon on the southern —each having two seconds with their weapons and armour.

Comail wore an open Roman helmet lined with cork, with a high crest, and jugulars fastened under the chin. His breast and back-plate were formed to the shape of the body, and the shoulder-pieces were hooked to rings in front. The lower part of the body was protected by the mitra, from which hung broad thongs covered with bronze scales. In his right hand he held a heavy javelin, and on his left arm was a round, hollow shield covered with steel plates, and having a Gorgon's head for a boss. At his left side hung a straight, heavy, two-edged Iberian sword, thirty inches in the blade and four inches wide in the widest part, having a sort of rib running to the point. On the right side this was balanced by a strong, well-tempered dagger.

Æscwine had a bright helmet, with a gilt boar's head and shoulders in the manner of a crest, and smaller figures of boars, inlaid in gold at the sides. This was worn over a hood of ringmail. The body armour was also of ringmail, very wide and loose, and came down to the knees. His shield was oblong, curved to the shape of a quarter of a cylinder. His sword was heavy, straight, and pointless; and he had a seax in his girdle. He also held a formidable spear, with a short point, in his right hand.

The seconds now went to the sides of the lists—a Briton and a Saxon on either side—and gave the signal for the fight to begin.

Each champion took a step forward, and with the full force of arm and body combined, sent their javelins spinning through the air. Æscwine's spear glanced from the rounded steel, burying its head in one of the stakes of the enclosure, and he caught Comail's weapon on the lower part of his shield, which was torn open, but no other damage was done.

Æscwine plucked out the dart, and sent it back at its owner, but like the first, it glanced from the smooth parma. Then both advanced into the centre of the ground, drawing their swords as they came on. The seconds, at the same time, drew their swords and closed up; Ælle pressed his horse's chest against the barrier, and the people stirred in their places as the shields clashed.

Crouching on their hams, the left shoulders well advanced, the men pressed their shields strongly together, and their eyes glared at each other over the rims, their right hands being raised and drawn back. At one and the same moment Æscwine made a cut at his adversary's leg, and Comail thrust at the face over against him. The spike of one shield was locked in the boss of the other, so that neither could guard quickly enough, and both were wounded. Then came a fierce rally, blows and thrusts being exchanged so quickly that the spectators could not easily follow them. It was several minutes before they reeled asunder, breathless and bleeding. Comail, accustomed to fight on horseback, had not sufficiently guarded his left leg, which was badly cut on the outside. Æscwine had lost his helmet, and the blood from several wounds in the head ran into his eyes.

It was agreed on both sides that the hurts should be bound up; but Æscwine was not allowed to resume his helmet as Comail had not lost any piece of armour, so the Saxon fought in his mail-hood.

This time they were somewhat less eager and guarded themselves more warily; so that Æscwine's blade, by striking often on the parma, lost its edge, and became but little better than a club. The heavy, well-tempered Spanish blade on the other hand had reduced the linden shield to such a wreck, that it was of little service to its bearer. Just as Æscwine flung away the shattered incumbrance, the sun looked over the hill top full in his eyes. He grasped the edge of the round shield with his left hand, dragging it down, and struck his antagonist so fiercely on the helmet as to fell him, stunned, to the earth; while Comail's broad point at the same moment entered the Saxon's shoulder, and rendered him incapable of holding a sword.

The seconds, seeing it was likely to be adjudged a drawn battle, moved by one impulse fell upon each other with such good will, that not having their shields, all four received serious wounds, whereof three—two Saxons and a Briton—presently died. This result was very grievous to the Saxons, for it is their wont to set some of their own men to fight an equal number of the enemy, each side armed after the manner of its own tribe, and the event shows the fortune of the campaign. When, therefore, they found that their men had rather the worst of it, they would fain have confounded the augury with a general fray, in which they hoped to get the upper hand. But it was not Ælle's policy to fight. These Britons were going away quietly, and every man who fell in a brawl with them was utterly wasted. It was necessary to make some concessions to the temper of the people, but further he would not go; so with much difficulty, and with the help of his chief men, he restored order, and drew off his reluctant troops.

While the foremost of them were leaving the ground, Farinmail's litter was brought to the spot where the king sat on his horse.

"Lord Ælle," said the young man, "this affair being settled, we are about to return to our own city. We thank you for your mansuetude in permitting this meeting, and in gracing it with your presence, and that of your companions. But our especial gratitude is due to the ladies who have deigned to honour us. If the Lady Ostrythe will accept this ring in perpetual memory of her beneficence, she will add a last favour to those for which I am already indebted to her, and which I despair of ever requiting as they deserve."

Ostrythe reined up her horse by the litter

and gracefully took the ring. She admired the chasing of the gold and the beauty of the engraved sardonyx which it enclosed; and assured Farinmail that she should never look at it without thinking of the giver, and of his noble courtesy.

There was one weak spot in Ælle's heart, where anything that concerned his children, especially Ostrythe, found ready entrance. He growled a little at Farinmail's speech, which savoured too much of the curling-tongs to please him. He felt in a blind sort of way that he would occupy a position of inferiority unless he met the young man with equal civility. When Ostrythe ceased speaking, he drew from his left arm a golden serpent of foreign workmanship, worth three hundred sheep, and leaning towards Farinmail, offered it, saying—

"It is not my custom to exchange aught but sword-strokes with my foes, but as we are not to meet again as enemies, at least for the present, I beg you to wear this in remembrance of your kindness to the daughter of Ælle, and so I bid you farewell."

"Thanks, and farewell, Lord King," cried Farinmail; but he still held Ostrythe's hand till her father was out of hearing. "Sweet lady!" he then continued, "I have one more request before we part, never probably to meet again. This serpent I shall wear with pleasure; but here is another ornament which will no more encircle my neck from this time," and he produced the golden torque allotted to him out of the spoil. "Your father lost this in the battle up yonder, and it was given to me. Some evening, when hearts are blythe, and men drink mead in the great hall, let the Lord Æscwine approach the king's high seat, restore to him the torque, and claim a reward for it. I wonder, I wonder what is the boon he will claim."

"Lord Farinmail," said Ostrythe, with a smile and a blush, and darkening eyes, "I could accept your gifts with more freedom if they were less costly. It is not for its own worth that we prize a jewel, it is the giver who makes it precious, and a trifle may outweigh a crown—a poor flower all the device of the goldsmith."

"Quite so," Farinmail replied. "A generous soul is indifferent whether the offering be of gold or of copper. Still we cannot help wishing to try, however feebly, to express the depth of our feeling and our gratitude. If you reflect that you saved me from being——"

"It was a jest, it was indeed," Ostrythe interrupted. "We do not eat people now, even as a religious exercise. It is quite a thing of past ages; when a man is sacrificed to the gods, other flesh is substituted at the feasts. You will soon be quite well now. Drink the willow bark and avoid swamps, and so I bid you farewell."

Ostrythe galloped after her father, while Farinmail, with his fellowship, set out on their return to Venta, and appear no more in this history.

The night had already fallen when Kynon re-entered the gate of Anderida, and he proceeded straight to his dwelling. Early on the morning of the duel, he went to the house of the Praefect, thinking it would be better to volunteer an account of his journey, than to run the chance of being asked about it. He gave a truthful statement of all that he had seen, adding, that there was nothing of any consequence going on, and that he was afraid to speak to the guides, as Ælle had expressly warned him against tampering with them, and the Saxon King did not seem to be one whose warnings might be disregarded with impunity. This made him chary of asking questions, and though he used his eyes, there was not much to be seen. He told of the men who were being paid, and spoke of certain ladders, remarkable for their great width. Julius asked many questions about these ladders, and seemed surprised that Kynon should have seen them where he did. After a few questions on other points, the medicus was dismissed, and met Bael at the door as he retired.

"Where do you come from now?" Julius asked, "and what news do you bring?"

"I have been at a fight—a single combat out yonder—cutting against thrusting. Thrusting with the point is very pretty, but too neat-handed for downright rough fighting. The Briton was cool and steady as one could wish, but at the first exchange, instead of hitting his man between the teeth, he struck between helmet and mail, the fastenings burst, and the boar's head rolled on the grass. At the last, instead of the throat, he pierced the shoulder, and the Saxon knocked him down like a man."

"I do not care about such details," Julius said, but the other went on—

"Then they were flinging javelins, mere reeds, not like this," and Bael took the pilum from the rack and poised the huge weapon with evident pleasure. It was nearly seven feet long, and three inches square at the stoutest part, the heavy steel head being prolonged half-way down the knotty cornel-shaft. On the opposite side of the peristyle was an old door, made of two-inch oaken plank, crossed vertically and horizontally. Bael threw himself back, the heavy spear flew with a "whew!" and buried itself for half its length in the stout planks, which continued to crack and rend for several seconds. It required a strong wrench to extricate the shaft, and as it came out, a sound of lamentation followed. It was not the voice of wounded Dryad, but of an unlucky slave, who passing down the lane had rested with his burden against the door. Bael applied his eye to the aperture he had made, and saw his victim binding up a slight wound in his thigh with a rag torn from his tunic, glancing still at the door.

"Ah! murderer!" cried the slave, and hurled a stone at the opening.

Bael withdrew in an unobtrusive manner, and replaced the pilum quietly in the rack, but the injured man kept up such a kicking and cursing, that some of Julius' people had to go out and beat him.

"Were the men of Gwent gone when you left?" the Praefect asked.

"They were going," Bael answered. "Farinmail was taking leave of Ælle, as it might be the parting of father and son. I guess the young one would not be sorry to marry the old man's daughter. That fellow who went out as I came in, was in the British camp yesterday, sneaking about like a dog who has stolen the butter."

"I sent him. Did you observe anything really suspicious?"

"He was riding with Smith—him who was prisoner here. They were as dumb as fishes as long as they were among the trees, but I could see they were talking earnestly when they got on to the open."

"It might be worth while to have him watched," Julius remarked.

"He is one of a sort that wants watching. He burrows like a mole. One can only tell where he is at work by the dirt he throws up?"

"He tells me there are scaling-ladders on the bridge, by the new tower."

"That is to make it appear that they are going to assault it, but it is my belief that they will try to burn it. The wood lying about there should be removed, and the remaining part of the bridge broken down, and mud heaped upon all the timbers not taken away."

"There is no time for that at present, the city has to be guarded, for a grand assault is impending. That tower is of no use to us now. I wish you to gain any information you can about the attack from above; no one can tell what may be important and what useless. The water should be watched at night; their boats will come seeking the best places to bring the ships to the walls."

"They have made preparations to attack on both sides," Bael said.

"I know it; but I think all the weak places are provided for by the new works. We must see that they do not cut the stakes."

"I will be on the water all night," Bael answered. "The signals will be the same as before, and I know where to find you."

Besides staking all the places where vessels of even the lightest draught could come near enough to the walls to lay their ladders, there were long iron-shod beams managed from above which seemed likely to prove a formidable obstacle to ships.

Wooden galleries also had been built out from the parapet where the space between the towers was too great. These were covered with green hides, and contained archers in the lower stage, while above two scorpions swept the wall to the right and left.

Bael had not been long gone when another visitor was announced. It was Renatus. The Praefect looked at the documents before him—lists of provisions accumulated here and there; accounts of the contents of various magazines of warlike stores; a proposal to deepen the wells, as the water was running short, demands for fresh timber for the works. He looked, and seemed half inclined to refuse an audience. But in such times it is dangerous to turn any one away; news may come from the most unexpected quarters, and the bearers of it are not unfrequently unconscious of the vital issues of their observation.

Renatus entered, aged and haggard, his eyes deeper set, and glowing with a fiercer fire than heretofore. His lean fingers twisted themselves together, or the hands moved in gestures which had no reference to his words, the movements seemed involuntary. The smooth utterance, the clear, silvery tones which had so often swayed thousands of hearers, were changed for harsh, feeble, jerking sentences, which usually ended with an unmeaning laugh.

"Well, Lord Praefect, working away as if the world were to last for ever. 'Spartam nactus es, hanc adorna;' though we agreed, I believe, once upon a time, that this city is not Sparta—ha, ha!"

"The world will last my time," Julius replied, "and while I last I must work. When do you start on your Frisian campaign?"

"I wish I could set out to-morrow—to-day.

There is nothing now to hinder my journey, the body is laid in the earth, the soul has departed to her doom; but I wander in a circle—ha, ha!"

"I can tell what detains you. You linger here to see the fulfilment of your prophecy. To-morrow is the forty-ninth day."

"No, no, the forty-eighth, not the forty-ninth; count again—again."

"I dare say you are right," said Julius carelessly; "but tell me, if the fatal day pass without disaster, if we survive to the fiftieth day shall we then be safe? Is the prediction tied up to the fixed date; or are we liable to ulterior pains, and postponed vengeance?"

"What do I know? Ask the conduit-pipe whether it pours forth water or wine, or bitter medicine. I deliver the message committed to me."

"You must have some knowledge of the intention or how can you choose the right words to use. Without accuracy the gift is valueless."

"The words are put into my mouth without choice of mine. They often have an interpretation entirely different from the one I suppose them to bear."

"What!" cried Julius, "an alternative meaning in case the more obvious one should miscarry. I thought the new oracles had forsaken those arts along with the shivering limbs, and starting eyes, and radiate locks of Pythia."

Renatus answered not, but looked far away, and Julius went on—

"How shall we know the true prophet from the impostor? How shall the man himself be sure that he is not the channel of his own pride or malice?"

"The event will show," the monk replied, slowly returning to the present.

"And you, a man of generous blood, a friend of the hero Vortimer, you are not ashamed to terrify the vulgar with these predictions, not being yourself assured of their truth till the event approve them."

"I said nothing of not being myself assured. The event is the proof to others.

Words are but feeble exponents of profound feeling, and rarely convey to others our whole thought and emotion. I seem to be in the condition of him who goes into the battle, sure that his cause is right, and just, and true; believing that it will triumph at last, but not knowing how this particular conflict will result, and very doubtful if he himself shall live to cry 'Victoria!' Does his foot turn aside, or his heart falter? Does he then review his reasons and arguments? The season is past for that work; the time now calls for swift and deadly strokes. In the fierce, raging strife, who stops to ask—Why am I on this side instead of that. Years ago I sought, inquired, and made my choice by the light of reason, of prayer, of faith; now with powers prematurely failing, harassed by Satan to the brink of frenzy and despair, I sustain the contest, I cling to hope, for 'I know in whom I have believed.'"

"Well," Julius said, "I suppose that is more or less the moral state of most men after a certain age. We cannot be always referring to first principles; certain axioms and postulates being granted, we know that certain truths can be established, but time is too short to be always repeating the proofs. The mischief is, that men pick out a few propositions and ignore others of co-ordinate quality. But as touching that forecast of yours—it is likely that to-morrow the question will be settled one way or the other. The Saxon preparations are made; they have about ten thousand men of one sort and another, and there seems no reason why the grand attack should be deferred. If clear brains, and stout hearts, and an old wall can break their strength, you may yet hear of victories as glorious as those of Vortimer."

The glow in Renatus' face was fading, but it lighted again at that name.

"Ah!" he exclaimed, "by the house of the ferry-boat there was fighting. Categirn was slain, and the first battle overthrown. But nothing could stand before Vortimer's charge. Horsa fell; Hengist turned and fled. I held the hero's hand in death, and wept on his grave by the sea. Had he lived, we should not be in these straits."

Julius returned to his work with compunctious feelings for the waste of time. Renatus wandered to the wall, and looked over the tide, thinking sadly, but not despondently, of old times, old deeds, old friends. By-and-by he went to an old house, and hunting in dusty places, found a rusty key, which, after several vain attempts, opened a quaintly-carved chest. In this he plunged his hands, feeling for some object. Then he took out the contents of the chest, garments, ornaments, scrolls, armour—dead limbs of a dying past—till he came to a dirty bundle, carefully tied up. This he unfolded, and took out a long dagger, Vortimer's last gift, and hid it under his frock, as if it might yet do service.

CHAPTER XII.

Ælle neglected nothing. He saw that many of his people were uneasy at the issue of the fight the day before, and knew that a feeling of being predestined to defeat might operate injuriously at that turning-point of the struggle, when both sides have had enough, each conscious of its own exhaustion, but ignorant of the condition of the foe. At such a time, when to hold out for another five minutes is victory, a small influence may have a great result, and an utterly unfounded statement that they are fated to win, may carry men over the perilous moments pregnant with triumph to one combatant—destruction to the other.

To counteract the baleful augury of yester-

ANDERIDA.

day, the king had recourse to sortilege; and desired Cnebba to arrange the lots in such wise as to promise success to the Saxon arms, and the plunder and destruction of a mighty fortress. But Cnebba was a true believer, and explained at large that the lots did not influence the event, but only foretold it; and that to tamper with them was not only wicked, but foolish; not ensuring success, and bringing the method into disrepute through failure.

Ælle listened patiently to the wise man, and when he had finished, sought another soothsayer, who, for a consideration, agreed to associate himself with Cnebba, and to take care that the lots gave a decided and favourable response to the inquiries of the faithful.

Cnebba chose a straight young branch of a plum tree, and divided it into eight pieces of equal length, which could not well be discerned one from another by the touch alone. Then he cut one side of each piece flat, taking care to remove the same quantity of wood and bark from each. He had prepared a sort of ink by mixing soot in water, thickened with plum-tree gum, and with this he marked the flat sides of the bits of wood, inscribing on each a sacred rune, singing the while verses in honour of the divinity whose mark he was making. As each was finished it was laid, wet side uppermost, in a box filled with sand, to be dried by the rays of the sun. The false seer, who had been appointed to assist Cnebba, squatted on the other side of the box, also muttering charms, and throwing his features into contortions most edifying to behold. In an absent manner, he from time to time took one of the lots from the box to see if it were dry, and contrived, without being observed, to cut a piece of bark with his sharp nails from those he intended to pick out afterwards. The three to be selected were, first the rune of Woden which promised victory to the Saxons, the rune of Thor which indicated the day, and that of Tiw which was supposed to favour the predominance of Ælle. A white cloth was spread over the grass; on one side stood Cnebba and his assistant, on the other the king with the chiefs and elders, while the people stood farther off, in a loose circle, showing eager interest.

Cnebba, with his face turned to the sky, advanced, uttering invocations, and scattered the lots at random on the cloth. Then the treacherous assistant, having been stripped and blindfolded to prevent foul play, was led to the edge of the cloth, and bidden to take up three of the lots. As he bent forward to feel for the pieces, a succession of shrieks outside the ring drew the attention of all in that direction. It was an old woman who had fallen down in a fit, and had to be carried away by two men. When the confusion occasioned by this incident was over, the false prophet picked up the lot nearest to him, and handed it reverently to Cnebba.

"The rune of Woden," cried Cnebba, handing the lot to the elders, who examined it and confirmed his statement, saying, "It is the rune of Woden."

"This," said Cnebba, "is the happiest of

runes, especially when it is the first to come up. It promises victory, honour, and vast spoil."

"This rune," he exclaimed, as he took the next, " belongs to Tiw."

" It is the rune of Tiw," said the elders, one after another.

" Tiw," said Cnebba, amid the approving gestures of the people, " is the father of Ælle the King. It is a happy lot, promising him success in the work he has in hand. Being the middle lot it tells of a great fire."

Taking the third lot, he said, in a loud voice, " This is the rune of Freá."

The assistant looked across to Ælle, frowning and shaking his head.

" I think that is a mistake," he said; " on that lot is the rune of Thor."

" You think I make a mistake," Cnebba said severely, passing the lot to the elders.

" It is the lot of Freá," said those into whose hands it first came.

" Freá tells us," Cnebba continued, with

his nose a little higher than before; "Fréa enjoins that the business before us shall be undertaken to-morrow. Coming last, this lot signifies the end of the war."

There was a joyful stir among the people, who were glad at the prospect of a speedy and triumphant return to their hearths.

Ælle meantime had beckoned to Ent, who stood in the front rank of the crowd, and whispered to him. The giant slipped away into the throng, and was quickly among the chiefs, reaching up to Smith's ear.

Smith held out his hand for the lot, and inspected it closely.

"What?" he asked with sternest countenance—"what is the punishment meted out for those who tamper with the lots sacred to the gods?"

An awed hush fell on the assembly, but Cnebba replied firmly—

"He is bound with cords on the altar of the god he has offended, his throat is cut by the priest, and his body burnt as a sacrifice."

"There is a mark on this lot," Smith said, "whereby it may be known."

But the false prophet had his wits about him, as it is very necessary that deceivers should have. He stepped forth before them all, and said—

"The penalty is for marking the lots before they are drawn; to mark them afterwards is no offence. I made a scratch on each as I took it up, that I might recognise it without fail if it were dropped by mischance. This practice has been delivered to us by them of old."

A violent debate ensued on this point, in which Cnebba's science and earnestness had great weight. Men looked at his nose—and believed.

After hot discussion, which brought to light the not unusual fact, that different customs prevailed in different places, the elders ruled that it was a doubtful case, and that the lots must be considered to have failed. Still the people were reminded that, so far as they had gone, the lots were unusually favourable, and that there was reason for confidence.

Ælle said that the best way to ascertain the will of the gods would be to attack to-day, when if they were unlucky it would be evident that the favourable omens were to take effect on the morrow.

"Lord King," Cnebba said in a low voice, "that fellow who was appointed to help me tried to falsify the lots. Let us rejoice that he failed, for the rune of Thor, coming last, signifies the death of a leader of men."

"Bother the runes," growled Ælle. "Say something to hearten the warriors."

Just then a vast cloud arose in the direction of the city.

"See," the king exclaimed, "already the sayings of the gods are fulfilling themselves. The great fire is to-day, whenever the rest may be."

The fact was, that Ent's first project for burning the new tower on the bridge had ended in smoke only, in consequence of the wetness of the materials. Fresh arrangements had been completed, and the king had bidden him, after giving a message to Smith, to apply fire.

The giant had disposed his combustibles with much art. Stacks of dry reeds, brushwood, and larger boughs had been built up under the broken bridge, with passages between them intended to lead the draught to the hollow of the tower, and make it serve as a great chimney. Ent, having carefully ascertained the direction of the wind, crept into his incendiary labyrinth, widened one opening, stopped another, struck a light, and hastily clapped his torch to the weather-side of the piles. Vapours curled about, flames darted from point to point, a dull roaring ran along the passages left for draught, till in a few minutes the vacant space under the bridge, where it was crossed by the tower, was a mass of white, rolling flame, like the hearth of a reverberatory furnace. Big beams and thick planking, which refused to ignite before a feeble attack, burned like kindling wood, and the upward rush of heated air carried aloft great blazing masses with myriad sparks. Ent watched till the heat became unbearable, making note of possible improvements.

Meantime those on the tower soon perceived the smell of burning, and found pungent vapour issuing from every crack in the lower part of the building. They gave the alarm, but the tide was low. It speedily became evident that the small quantities of water they could throw on the fire had no effect in quenching it; indeed, some asserted that the fluid seemed to feed the flame. Julius had resolved not to waste strength in defending this point, which no longer served as an outlet, and had removed the military engines and other valuable matters. When the conflagration was reported to him, he ordered the garrison to be withdrawn, and the boats which filled up the broken part of the bridge to be removed without delay.

Ælle spent the morning in a careful inspection of the preparations on board ships and boats. The fleet was to attack from the south, and the new boats mounted with ladders were appointed to assail the northern face. The king soon perceived that it would be useless to fit up many of the vessels with ladders, as the points at which the walls could be approached with any chance of success were few, and the obstructions at these spots were so formidable that not many could be made accessible in the short time available, a period not exceeding half an hour on each side of high water. Ladders not in position by three quarters of an hour after high tide, which would be about four hours after noon, could never be laid to the wall till another sun rose.

The first squadron was to consist of boats roofed over with strong baulks of timber, the roof being covered with a stratum of earth. These had the duty assigned them of clearing away the impediments placed by the citizens to block the way to the wall.

The second division was formed of ladder-boats, which were to be warped in when the covered boats had cleared the way for them, a space of seven yards being allowed from the foot of the ladder to the base of the wall, when the top rung rested on the summit. The last division consisted of flat-bottomed barges on the northern side, and the ships of the fleet on the other, from which a continuous stream of men would flow to the ladders when planted.

On the eastern side of the city, where the land was highest, Julius had reared, above one of the towers, a wooden structure twenty feet high, the summit being nearly sixty-five feet above high-water mark. From this elevation the eye ranged over the flat country, and plunged into many a recess of the woods. Here a watchman was stationed, relieved at intervals of three hours, from dawn till twilight ended, and hither Julius often came, trusting rather his own senses than any other.

He too had been visiting every post, examining every possible landing-place, looking to the firmness of stakes and beams, inspecting the various military engines, and seeing that each had an adequate supply of missiles. At frequent points along the parapet were handcarts with stores, from which archers and slingers might supply themselves when they ran short. He had also reviewed all the bodies of fighting men in the city, addressing them in a short, hearty speech. He told them that the Saxons had not the military skill requisite to take a fortress like Anderida, unless they found some one inside to open the gate. Brute force can never take a fortress guarded by walls like these, so long as the defenders have food, and do their duty like men and Britons.

"You will fight to-day for life, for your own existence, and that of your wives and little children. If any man's heart and strength flag in the bitter conflict, let him think of the fate of Regentium, and nerve his hand for one more blow. You can and will beat back the host of Ælle this day. Succours will arrive ere long, and when the full power of the realm is united, it is not in these barbarians to make head against it."

The men believed his words, and went away cheerfully to their midday meal.

About noon Julius mounted to the watch-tower, to look out for any signs of activity in the Saxon fleet, which must of necessity begin to move soon, if it intended to fight to-day. He had not been long at his post, when boats were seen putting off from the northern division, which would have the tide against it. The boats seemed to be laying out kedges, by means of which the heavier craft might warp themselves off the mud as it was thinned by the rising water. Soon shouts of men, hauling together, were faintly heard, and one dark object after another glided from under the shadow of the trees, formed a line with others, and came slowly sweeping and towing in the direction of the city. The fleet, which lay under the land toward the south-east, remained at rest. The larger vessels required a higher rise of the tide, which, instead of impeding, would help their advance to the wall.

Julius leaned on the rail which ran round

the platform, and let his mind ramble without control. He knew better than to keep up the tension needlessly. Even when resting, his fancy did not wander far from its usual limits. It flew, first to the west, wondering what the Pendragon was doing. Was he aware of the danger to which the fortress was exposed? Was he too hard bested? Would help come in time to save a bulwark that could never be replaced? As the city was hemmed in by the barbarians, so Julius was isolated by the ignorance of those about him. There was no congenial friend, whose sympathetic tastes and habits could beguile the intervals of a tedious round of petty functions. Here, however, was his station, duty which he could not forsake till the 'missio honesta' came; and he knew full well through what a grisly messenger the honourable discharge would reach him.

By this time Cymen's ships were rippling the shining water with steady oar-strokes; the heat was too fierce for unnecessary toil, and the tide rowed in their stead. They came nearer, and the boats from the northern division were within range of the engines on the wall, when the Praefect bid a trumpeter sound the "classicum." The man advanced his right foot, poising himself chiefly on the left, then, with head thrown back, and right hand near the bell of the long tube, he blew a clear, swelling note, ending with a taratantara, which rang over waters a league away.

A red flag was run up on the staff of the highest tower of the palace; a clanking and clash of steel sounded in the intervallum below, and the soldiers came running up the stone steps which led to the top of the wall. Some were buckling their sword-belts, some bracing their shields, others fastening the thongs of the helmet or hooking the shoulder-pieces to the breast-plate. They thronged the parapet, stumbling, jostling, cursing, jesting; but very quickly settling into their places, and into silence.

The machines began their horrible din, missiles whistled or hurtled in the air, and yells of men mingled with the thud and crash of riven wood. Julius expected that the ladders would be planted first on the northern side, but he hesitated now, seeing that the ships of the fleet no longer carried their old arrangement, but brought only hand ladders.

Cymen had been warned by the exploring parties that the obstructions were too solid to be destroyed in the time at their disposal, and it had been resolved to bring in the ships close to the stakes, and land in boats.

The Praefect sent orders to those in charge of the engines, to direct all their efforts to the destruction of these light skiffs which passed over or between the obstacles. When these could go no farther, the men in them jumped overboard, and waded through mud and water, holding their shields over their heads in a slanting direction. In spite of the slaughter, the space at the foot of the wall was soon filled. Ladders were passed ashore, and elevated without much difficulty, but as they approached the parapet, great beams, hung on shears, were swung round, which striking them on the side, knocked them over.

All this time the engines continued their deadly work. Rows of men were knocked over by a single missile, ships were shattered and sank, boats were crushed with their crews; beams and stones broke the tortoise-like shield array, and hot sand and boiling water found joints in the harness.

Cymen and some others went round one of the towers to a part of the wall less vigilantly guarded; they raised a ladder before those above could prevent it, rushed up, and after a sharp struggle gained a footing on the summit. The Ætheling turned to the side where Julius stood, and fought his way toward the silver eagle. The Britons gave way before the fiery sailor; they were slain or thrown into the intervallum. A dart from a scorpion struck the Ætheling in the throat, pierced the ringmail and the neck through and through, and he fell back mortally wounded. His companions threw themselves before their chief and friend, locked their shields, and broke the onset of the Britons.

Eormenred, with a few men, had not followed Cymen, but turned along the wall in the opposite direction. Here he was met by Etlym Redsword and Cadogan. Eormenred fell upon the latter, and beat him back with blow upon blow. Etlym encountered one of the Beorlafingas, and killed him suddenly, before he could raise his shield. Eostrewine sprang to avenge his kinsman, and fell with a deep wound in his side. Esné struck the Briton so sharply that he staggered back, though his well-tempered helmet turned the blow. Then the outlaw dropped his sword and shield, picked up the wounded lad, and tried to carry him to the ladder. Several deep stabs he got, for Madoc brought up some scores of men, and drove the Saxons back. Eormenred and Bosa, with the other Beorlafingas, fought to cover his retreat, and the Saxons, who were carrying off the body of the Ætheling, met them at the ladderhead. Esné scrambled on to the highest rung, holding his burden on his left arm and shoulder in such wise that he could grasp the sides of the ladder. He slid swiftly to the ground, and fell all of a heap at the bottom, with Eostrewine upon him, and moved not again.

Above, some desperate fighting was going on, the odds against the Saxons increasing every moment. Eormenred came down without sword or buckler, but the blood of Etlym was red on his seax. He soon found his boy, fetched water in his helmet, and dashed it over the lad's face. Eostrewine opened his eyes, flung his arms round his father's neck, kissed the blood-spotted cheek, sobbed " for the mother," and fell back dead. Bosa came down and dragged Eormenred to a boat; the body of the Ætheling was brought down by two of his companions—the rest of them died in their ranks, as was right, when their chief was killed. They slew many Britons, among whom was Madoc, who lay beside Etlym and Cadogan.

Long before this time, Julius, perceiving

that there was no danger here, had gone round to the northern side, where Ælle's attack was in progress. The stakes had been removed by light boats, which came in as soon as the depth of water permitted, and fixed a tackle to the head of each stake, by means of which the crew of a vessel, securely moored at a short distance, pulled out the stakes or broke them. This work took time, and it was the top of high water before three vessels got in close to the wall, and let fall their ladders. The men mounted at once, but on reaching the summit, found a large shutter raised in their faces, which barred all access to the platform. They pushed and hammered with hilt, and hacked with sword-blade, but made little progress till Thorsten the tall came up with his axe-men, and speedily split two of the screens into chips.

Ælle, as soon as he came to the ladders, threw planks from boat to boat, and made a strong platform on which to draw up his Gesithas. These advanced in long double lines to the foot of the ladders, holding their shields so that they made a kind of roof, overlapping each other like tiles.

At this stage of the fight Julius came to the northern side, and at once ordered fireballs and pitch-pots to be thrown at the vessels and ladders.

Thorsten leaped from the topmost rung as the screen before him gave way, and smote Meredith's head in twain; but Laelius stabbed him as he raised his hand for a second blow, and the straight Roman blades of the city guard made short work of the axes.

Ælle made his appearance at the head of one ladder, and Brorda at the other, and four hundred Gesithas were behind them mounting or ready to mount. Darts, arrows, and stones at such short range, made terrible havoc; and the earthen vessels, which broke and covered the men with blazing pitch, were not pleasant to face. It was not the men Julius wished to burn, but the ladders, and already wood smoke mingled with the pitchy vapours; even the boats, covered with wet hide, began to kindle.

Five of the city guard set upon the Saxon King; and Laelius found himself in front of Brorda. The Saxon was the more powerful man, but the captain of the guard was an accomplished swordsman, and pierced his antagonist through the eye to the brain. The Gesithas ran up the two ladders and freed Ælle, who straightway turned upon Laelius, striking the Briton's shield with his own till he beat it down. Then the king made a downright cut at his foe. The sword glanced from the polished helmet, but shore through shoulder-plates and collar-bone down to the region of the heart, and the cousin of Julius fell dead.

Ælle was still tugging to extricate his sword, when Wyverth the Gesith pushed up to him, and whispered in his ear—

"The two ladders we came up by are burnt through and fallen. No more men can join us from below. The ships also are burning fiercely."

"Make for the third ladder," Ælle said, "and get them up that way."

As he spoke the sword came out suddenly, and the king staggered back. The bishop, who was mounting the steps of the platform, bearing in his hand a heavy iron-bound crozier, smote the king therewith on the head, so that he fell stunned on the stones. Wyverth took the fallen man by the shoulders, Sæbald grasped the knees, and bore him toward the remaining ladder, while the rest of the Gesithas rallied round them, frantic for revenge. Wulfhere with the club, the youngest but one of the company, saw the king fall, and stabbed the bishop under the breast-bone right through the body, and he died. The shutter in front of the third ladder was easily torn down from the inside, when the props and stays were knocked away. No fresh men came up; the vessels not sunk or burnt were hauling off from these fatal walls. Wyverth, Sæbald, and Wulfhere carried the king down the ladder, hailed a small boat, and rowed to the ships. None of the other companions followed, they stood near the head of the ladder, that their lord might not be pursued. They held the Britons at bay for some time, till Bael broke their ranks with his terrible axe, and the city guard cut them to pieces.

Ælle soon came round when his helmet was removed, and eagerly inquired how things had gone on the other side of the city. The answers were unsatisfactory, but nothing certain was known at present.

Two boats were approaching the ship where the king lay under an awning, which shielded him from the afternoon sun. Ostrythe and Eanfled sat in the stern of one, the other carried Ceolwulf and Brihthelm. This latter reached the gangway first, and after a few words shoved off again to meet the ladies. When they came near—

"The king is safe," Brihthelm said, "but we bring him ill news."

"That you have failed?" said Eanfled. "We shall win another time."

"You have lost heavily," Ostrythe observed. "It is sad, but cannot be helped."

"I wish," old Ceolwulf said, in a shaky voice, for he loved the reckless Ætheling—"I would that we had lost twice as many, so that one had been saved. He was not with us; we never got on to the wall. He did, and was killed by one of those accursed machines. Lady, we wish you to tell Ælle; you will do it better than we."

"You speak of my brother?" Ostrythe asked, trembling.

Ceolwulf nodded, and she bent her head on her hands, and her shoulders shook with deep sobs. Presently she uncovered her face, and pointed to the vessel where her father was.

The men looked at her with pitiful eyes, and touched the water gently, as if they feared their oars might hurt it.

Ostrythe went under the awning, keeping her back to the light.

"Dear father, you are safe. How are you feeling now?"

"A little stupid and confused; well enough otherwise."

"Are you well enough, strong enough, to hear bad news?"

"Always well enough for that. Never keep back ill news. When a man knows the worst, he will often find that it may be amended."

"This cannot be amended." Then she sank on her knees by the rough couch, laid her cheek on her father's hand, sobbed out the name of Cymen, and wept passionately.

Ælle did not move, except to place his other hand on his daughter's head, till the storm abated. Then he asked for details.

Ostrythe told all she knew. When it was done, Ælle said—

"You must not be weak. He fell like a man, and like a man I will avenge him. That soothsayer spoke truly, and the rest of his speech shall be fulfilled. The means are ready to my hand."

"I suppose," said Ostrythe, "that they have sisters too."

"Before the sun rise to-morrow there shall be neither sister nor brother, father nor child.

May the utmost wrath of gods, and scorn of men, fall and rest on me if I spare one living thing.

And so Ælle went to Ceolwulf and Brihthelm, and arranged matters with them; also he sent for Smith and Ent. All men soon became aware that something of unusual interest was about to take place; and to the many who had lost kinsman or friend, the very air seemed to whisper " revenge."

THE END.

Rhys sat gasping by the grated window through the hot day, watching pertinaciously for the messenger who should bring him to examination and release. The sun shone on the upper steps of the pit, and the right-hand side of the descent was in shadow, which crept slowly round to the east.

The tramp of men mustering for defence, the loud trumpet-blast, the rush to the wall, these sounds were followed by a hush, soon to be broken by the jarring dissonance of the engines, and the yelling hand-to-hand struggle which swelled, shifted place, and died away. To these succeeded other noises— the clearing of the wreck, when the sanguinary storm was overpast.

Darkness came on, and weariness, and thirst, after the toil and excitement of the day; and before midnight, sleep and silence held the city in their soft grasp. Only the wounded kept vigil, and they who watched by the wounded.

The night was sultry, and Rhys sat in the same place, his head resting against the rusty, cobwebbed bars, his mind in a torpid state, as when a man cannot be sure whether he has slept or not; when time elapses unmeasured, and thought unremembered.

There was a bustle at the top of the steps; lights gleamed redly on slimy walls and, flashing between the dungeon bars, woke the sordid sleepers.

Aron and the slave came down, each holding a torch, pushing before them a savage-looking outcast whose face was stiff with half-dried blood. Midway, the jailer bid his prisoner get on, with a curse and a push which sent the heavily ironed wretch headlong to the bottom.

The rusty bolts and locks and lumbering

bars made noise enough to rouse the seven men of Ephesus, and woke the poor captives from forgetfulness. Heaven alone knows what visions of relief it had sent to the dreamers of this infernal cave. Perhaps they were leaping for joy in the free air of the bondless ocean, or climbing the untamed mountains, when cursing and fetter-clank recalled them to their foul and choking den. A growl of meaningless execration from the end of the vault stirred the jailer's bile. He snatched a heavy whip from behind the door, and stalked into the inner gloom with torch and scourge, a very minister of Tisiphone.

The sound of the lash and the howls of the victims rang in the arched roof till Aron returned, cutting right and left, in mere wantonness of tyranny. One snarled a wish of vain fury; whereupon the jailer turned and thrashed the fellow till arm and breath alike failed him.

A slight rattle behind made him turn quickly, but too late. The prisoner, waiting to be shackled, swung his clasped hands round his head, and brought the long links which united them crash on the jailer's left temple. Aron fell between two prisoners who fastened upon him with teeth and claws, but he was a powerful man and made a good fight, till the heavy irons, falling on his head again and yet again, like forge hammers, stretched him on the stones a moaning, insensible mass.

The slave stood by the door perfectly apathetic, till his master was subdued. Then a thought seemed to cross his dull brain. He looked at Rhys, took a small key from a hook, unlocked the shackle, dragged his benefactor out, and fastened the door.

"Why not leave it open," Rhys asked, "and let them escape?"

"We two can steal away unseen. Such a lot as these would rouse the watch at once. What have they done for me?"

This was unlooked-for wisdom, but a fool usually knows his own business.

They went quietly to the lodge, where the slave punched out the rivets of fetters and manacles, and Rhys stretched his limbs with a sensation of almost forgotten happiness. The slave asked what should be done.

"If I could get on the roof unobserved, the rest would be easy."

"I can find the way on to the roof," said the slave.

They found some of Rhys' wine, which Aron had been drinking when the malefactor was brought in. A horn apiece gave them renewed strength. They gained the roof, and stole across with precautions which were needless, as there was no one to interfere with them.

Julius himself had posted the guards and visited them at midnight, but he could not be everywhere. Laelius was slain, many chiefs had fallen, and those who succeeded to their authority had been drinking their own and their friends' luck, secure that the attack could not be renewed at present. The men did as the officers, and were asleep or absent.

Rhys and his companion left the palace at the spot where Ostrythe made her escape, and went along the intervallum toward the postern, that being the shortest way to the street in which he lived.

Opposite the postern, lying in the ray of light which streamed from the open door of the guard-chamber, was a man who called feebly for help. Rhys, stooping, saw that it was Kynon, badly wounded. The medicus, partly by words, partly by signs, instructed his friend to take a small packet from his breast, unfasten it, and put part of its contents in his mouth. In a little time he revived, and said—

"The mad monk stabbed me;—said I was a devil in body of a Saxon he slew by a ferry. All drunk in guard-chamber. Smith outside."

Rhys, delighted at the prospect of meeting Smith, ran to the guard-room. As he took the keys, it struck him that two of the men must have been very drunk to go to sleep in such strangely uncomfortable postures, but there was no time for searching into it.

The slave raised Kynon to a sitting

position, so that he could look about him. A queer look, half smile, half scowl, came over the features of the dying medicus as Rhys opened the first door, and disappeared under the vault to unfasten the outer one.

Rhys came back, but not as he went. Smith's strong hand was on his arm, and the Saxon seemed to speak reassuringly to him. Behind Smith was Ælle, grim as a War-god, and behind Ælle the whole available strength of the Gesithas. Up they came, stalwart young fellows, and filed off, right and left, to seize the steps leading from the intervallum to the summit of the wall, killing guards and sentries before they had time to raise an alarm. The king gave the word, "Slay, and spare not!"

Kynon's half smile stiffened into a grin, but his glazing eyes still seemed to watch with satisfaction the number and bearing of the avengers.

The Gesithas had passed. Cymen's sailors were entering now. It was easy to see by their looks, as the word was repeated to the leader of each section, that their hands would not be slack to avenge the Ætheling. The first party of these was sent to the right to seize the Decuman gate; the second went straight to the Forum and Basilica; the third turned to the left, with orders to make themselves masters of the palace. Not till all the points of vantage were in his hands, would Ælle allow the signal to be given.

The command concerning the palace seemed to awake Rhys from a dreamy state. He struggled to free himself from Smith's clutch.

" Shall I let him go ? " Smith asked. " He has a little private grudge to settle. I will be surety for him. We owe him something for his service."

" Who cares for the sticks when the logs are alight ? " Ælle replied.

Smith put his own interpretation on this oracular answer, and let Rhys go.

The grey light was by this time strengthening in the east, a brisk fresh air breathed coolness from the sea, dispelling the sultry closeness of the night. Ælle bit his dew-soaked moustache, and beat the stones with his heel impatiently, waiting for the blast that was to tell of the opening of the great gates. The time seemed long, though really only a few minutes. A deep roar from the horn of the Ætheling's signalman woke the sleepers of the city, bidding them pay the price of his blood.

Rhys ran, but those he followed had such a start that he could not pass them. He turned aside to his own house, snatched a light ladder, passed out the back way, and mounted at the spot whence he had descended an hour before. As he did so the horn rang out, but its deep note was drowned in the shouting and battering at the palace gates, which gave way, one after another, with crashing noise. Rhys hurried from terrace to terrace, but was obliged to stop for breathing space, and picked up a bar of iron before starting afresh. The Saxons were not yet come to the housetops, they were firing the lower rooms, and cutting down the occupants as they rushed out in distraction. Rhys pushed on among naked, shrieking creatures running to and fro, mad with fear. He thought he had missed his quarry, and stood facing the east, scanning the frenzied groups with dry-mouthed excitement.

A woman, with streaming hair and starting eyes, ran toward him—

"Rhys! Rhys! save me!" she cried, but recoiled from the expression of his face, and crouched, hiding her face in her hands, the thick locks covering her like a cloak. So the Saxons found her.

There! there at last was the man he sought; forsaken, forgotten, sobered by fright, shivering, helpless. Rhys went to him, and took his arm. Iorwerth made no resistance, but as they went along muttered—

"You are good. You will save me. I will make you rich."

They came to a room, from which light curls of smoke issued. Rhys led his captive in, knocked him down, and fastened the door with the iron bar, brought a stool, and sat calmly by the prostrate wretch. There was a trampling outside, flight and pursuit, dull blows and cries. Some one tried to burst open the door, but was called away. Then all was quiet but for an occasional moan.

Thicker and thicker rolled the smoke, flickering flames showed in corners. Iorwerth made a convulsive, choking effort to rise, but Rhys pressed him down with heavy foot, and hummed—

> "Ah, hate may watch with love, sweetheart,
> And death peer in between."

Neither stirred after this, and very soon afterwards the floor fell in.

Howel Hên was quickly afoot and armed. He roused his grandson, and bid him try to escape with Bronwen. The old man gathered as many of the palace guards as could be found; put Vortipore, who was still feeble, in a litter, and prepared to sally forth, so that if nothing better could be done, at least they might die sword in hand.

Howel the younger made his way to

the women's court, and after some difficulty found Bronwen. This court was the farthest from the gates, and the Saxons had not yet found their way into it; but the wreaths of smoke, the shouts, the yells of agony, had penetrated there, and sufficiently alarmed the inmates. Bronwen consented to fly with her lover, and, in spite of her terror, showed herself far more ready-witted than he. She wrapped herself in a grey cloak, and caught up some showy jewels to throw in the pursuers' way if they should be hard pressed.

The nearest way to the garden-door, by which they hoped to escape, was impeded by numbers of terrified women, so they went round by the terrace, which overlooked the main court of the palace.

A tumult down below attracted their notice, and they paused for a moment to look over. Howel Hên, with about forty of the guard, was making a gallant attempt to cut his way to the gate. The first charge found the Saxons scattered and unprepared, and the Britons forced their way, slaughtering to the centre of the square. But the enemy came swarming upon them in ever-increasing numbers, and now the guards were giving ground. Closer and closer they came to the wall, where Bronwen stood as if turned to stone, her hand pressed against her throat to keep down an hysteric choking. Vortipore knew that his hour was come, bid the men set down his litter, and picked up a sword. His darling's voice reached his ear; he looked up, smiled, and waved a last adieu. Then he pushed to the side of Howel Hên, who was fighting bare-headed now, the blood dripping from his white curls. Still the old man caught the blows deftly on his shield, and repaid them with adroit and deadly thrusts.

Her father's smile reminded Bronwen of the night, not long ago, when the Count feasted in the hall with his chiefs, when the harpers harped and sang, and she handed him the cup as he caressed her hair.

It was but a flash of memory, a momentary vision. Just then came a fierce rush, the ranks were broken, the Britons trodden underfoot, Vortipore was gone, Howel Hên's white curls were seen no more ; men stooped and rose again, each wiping a bloody seax, and the cry went up—

"Cymen the Ætheling! Slay, and spare not!"

Bronwen stepped upon the low parapet, gathered her cloak closely round her, and sprang into the medley below.

Julius had retired to rest after posting the guards at midnight. He had noticed the deficiencies both in numbers and watchfulness of those who were relieved, but was compelled to admit excuses, the truth of which he had no means of testing. It was annoying, but there was no remedy for it to-night, and he determined to go the rounds again a little before the third watch was set, and mark those who were negligent. The whole system would require reconstruction, the loss of officers had been so great. Accustomed to wake when he would, the Praefect opened his eyes and looked at the clepsydra. It was not yet time; he might take a few minutes more, and sleep was precious. A few sharp cries reached his ears —such sounds were common. He thought—

"More cases for to-morrow. I must have a deputy for the tribunal."

He was hardly asleep when Bael came in, and shook his patron's arm.

"There are sounds in the city of bodies of armed men moving about. I cannot tell the direction inside these walls. The clients are arming, and it would be well to send and call out the city guard."

"Is it so serious?" Julius asked. "The people are fatigued."

"I hear movements of men stepping together, and at times the clash of armour. It has been going on for some minutes. Come out here."

Julius went into the garden of the peristyle, buckling his breastplate as he went, but could hear nothing. He knew the keenness of Bael's senses, and bid him find out what caused the mysterious noises.

Julius called a slave, and was soon completely armed. His hand rested by accident on the silver eagle as the man fastened his boots. Bael came in quickly, but with no sign of emotion, sent away the slave, and said—

"The Saxons are in the city. Two hundred of them crossed in front but now, going to the great gates. They are also on the walls in some places. I can save you, if you care to escape."

Julius sighed; his work was frustrated after all. However, it was his to perform the task appointed him, regardless of the result.

"Send messengers to call out the city guard. Bid them come by the narrow lanes. I shall clear the Forum for them to meet in."

"Then you do not care to save your life for work hereafter."

"My work is here, and now. He who despairs cannot win. Shall a man do his duty strenuously all his life and shrink at last?"

An officer came and announced that the

clients and a few of the city guard, some sevenscore in all, were drawn up and ready.

"How could I abandon these?" said the Praefect going out.

"I did not suppose you would," Bael replied, "but it was proper to give you the choice. Now, Heavenly Lord, look after these thy weapons, for I, the last of thy children, am going to my last fight. Woods for brave men; walled places are but traps."

Bael grasped the heavy pilum as well as his axe and shield and, following Julius, took his place beside the eagle.

At that moment the horn roared its signal from the Decuman gate, and a horrible outcry resounded all round the walls. A wounded officer of the city guard came up, and told Julius, with failing breath—

"The sentries were asleep. We were surprised in our quarters. The great gates are open; the Saxons coming in eight men abreast."

It wanted yet about an hour to the sunrise, which few should live to see. One after another a few men of the city guard ran up and took their places.

"Do not let this fall into the hands of barbarians," Julius said, touching the eagle. Bael nodded, and the classicum sounded.

The mobbed Saxons were no match for these serried files, and the little band, with dripping blades, swept across the square to the Basilica.

The church was burning, the street was in flames, the view was bounded by smoke pillars bending in the sea-breeze, and hiding the palace.

"We might get to the west postern up that street to the right," one said.

"And then—— ?" asked Julius, "However, there is nothing better to be done."

Renatus was discovered sitting with his back to the wall, dead Saxons in front of him.

"The end is come," Julius said. "The event justifies the prophet."

"The end of chaos and delusion," Renatus answered with weak voice: "the beginning of order and life. But how did these hordes find an entrance? Have you admitted the Trojan horse within the walls?"

" I know not," Julius replied, "at least we have received the horse of Seius."*

Renatus' voice failed, but his lips moved. Julius stooped to catch the words, and when he raised his head, the sign of the cross was marked in wet blood on the forefront of his helmet.

For the last time in these parts the Roman charging call was blown. High it pealed above the tumult of the sack, the shouts of men, the screams, the roaring flames, the crashing walls and timbers, rising above them as an eagle dominates the lesser fowl. Its voice reached the Saxon King, who sent fresh troops to answer the haughty challenge. It fell on the surdescent ears of John and Eleutherius as it were the trumpet of doom.

* Equum Seianum recipere. Seius had a fine horse, which after his death passed into various hands, but whoever obtained it was ruined. Hence, to have the horse of Seius, became a proverb for ill luck.

The stiffening limbs of veterans quivered with a last attempt to answer the well-known summons.

Reformed on a narrower front, the Britons charged again. The Saxons, with locked shields, stretched across the Forum. Bael transfixed one with the pilum, and swinging his axe right and left broke through the line. The Britons turned to the right, driving their foes in heaps with heavy loss, till they came to the opening of the street where the house of Rhys stood. Here they were compelled to face about and show front to Witgar and the Jutes of Kent, who, with a party of sailors headed by Ceolwulf, fell on their rear. The growing light was eclipsed by a dark pall of smoke, advancing from the eastern quarter of the city. By the light of burning houses, the Britons might be seen closing up their ranks and giving death for death.

Julius, wounded, leaned with both hands on the eagle, before which Bael stood, smiting on this side and on that. Witgar sprang forward to grasp the staff, but fell with Bael's axe in his brain. Ceolwulf, with four of his crew, made a rush and cut down Julius, but his skull was shattered by a backstroke, and the sailors shared his fate.

Three hundred bodies cumbered the entrance of the narrow street. Bael stood alone over the corpse of his friend and patron, bleeding from a score of wounds, catching the blows aimed at him on the tough staff of the eagle, and returning them. Few who came within the sweep of those long strong arms needed a second stroke.

A sword cut severed the cornel shaft, and Bael, stooping to recover the silver emblem, got his death wound. With a final effort he flung axe and eagle far away into a blazing ruin, laughed grimly to see how completely the wall of fire encompassed his assailants, and fell—the last of the men of Anderida!

All the eastern end of the city was solid fire, which swept rapidly round by the intervallum, where the air was freer than in the narrow lanes.

The conflagration spread with doubled and redoubled swiftness as it grew in volume; the heat sucked in the air, and the wind fanned the flames.

The intense glow seemed to draw from all combustible things some inflammable essence, through which fiery tongues leaped fathoms long, and lines of buildings burst at once into a blaze. A huge pillar rolled upward, cloud-like, and bent far streaming down the wind. Leagues away people looked with fear, wondering what the sign might portend.

The Saxons ran down the street they had so far cleared, only to find a raging barrier at the end—a fearful arch of triumph for the conquerors. Some held their shields before their faces and attempted to rush through the furnace; some tried to escape in other directions, only to involve themselves in smoke-blind labyrinths, and perish by their own design.

Ælle withdrew his men from the walls, contenting himself with keeping watch at the

Decuman gate, while boats rowed guard upon the waters. High tide and sunrise came together that morning, and at the half-ebb it was no longer needful to wait.

His vow was fulfilled. No living thing came forth.

The Saxon camps were broken up, the fleet sailed, the army marched westaway, the work was done. No joyous song, no shout of victory, cheered their homeward course. The accomplishment of their purpose had been dearly bought, the blod-wit was heavy and sore. From the king downward, scarce a family but mourned its slain. There were fields which bore nought but weeds, there were ships that lay splitting in the sun for many a year.

Worst lot of all to bear was theirs who were uncertain of the fate of their friends. One had seen them here, another there, then the trace was lost. Autumn succeeded to summer, hoary winter came, and still hope sickened in hearts which could not endure to let it go.

The reek of Anderida was fit incense to the fierce deities of a fierce race; grim gods who loved the sacrifices of the sword.

A milder religion overspread the land, numbering, among its later conquests, the South Saxons. The desolate site remained as a forsaken altar—a witness of the merciless past.

The Roman walls stood, defiant as ever, and forest creatures crouched beneath their shadow. The fox yelped at night among the fallen stones, the owl hooted from a hollow in the wall. Seeds grew to trees with wide-sheltering branches, and voices, as of the dead, shrieked and groaned from the boughs their bones had nourished. Fowler or fisherman seldom troubled the waters, which silently shrank from the waste chester.

Name and story were alike forgotten.

Other storms of conquest beat upon the shore, and the spoiler in turn bowed his neck to the harsh yoke.

Sea became land, and dry land sea, as age

after age went by in long procession, with war and tempest, and corroding change.

Through every chance the ancient wall endures; even now we see—meet tokens of the masters of the world; wasted by man, crowned by time—the steadfast towers of Anderida.

THE END.

www.ingramcontent.com/pod-product-compliance
Lightning Source LLC
Chambersburg PA
CBHW032054220426
43664CB00008B/994